THE BEATLES COMPLETE SCORES

THE BEATLES COMPLETE SCORES

WISE PUBLICATIONS
LONDON / NEW YORK / PARIS / SYDNEY / COPENHAGEN / MADRID

Exclusive Distributors
for
European Economic Community,
Australia and New Zealand:
Music Sales Limited,
8/9 Frith Street,
London W1V 5TZ,
England.
Music Sales Pty Limited,
120 Rothschild Avenue,
Rosebery, NSW 2018,
Australia.

Order No. NO90548
ISBN 0-7119-3293-X

Exclusive Distributors
for
United States of America
and Canada:
Hal Leonard Publishing Corporation
7777 West Bluemound Road
P.O. Box 13819
Milwaukee, WI 53213

ISBN 0-7935-1832-6
HL00673228

Transcription by Tetsuya Fujita, Yuji Hagino, Hajime Kubo and Goro Sato.

Book design by Pearce Marchbank Studio, London.
Cover photograph by David Redfern.
Frontispiece photograph by Don McCullin/Magnum.

Printed in the United States of America.

A GUIDE TO THE MUSIC

A great deal of effort has been put into presenting these performances in musical notation that is as faithful as possible to the original recordings.
Due to the limitations inherent in transcribing sounds into notes there are a number of suitable nuances and rhythms that are impossible to express in print.
It is recommended, therefore, that you carefully listen to the recordings in order to gain a feel for the sounds that these musical symbols represent.

Note that the male vocal parts, as well as the parts for guitar and bass, are written an octave higher than they sound on the records.
On the other hand, the piano parts, as well as other keyboard instruments, are all written in the same octave as they sound on the recordings.

GUITAR

C – bend
U – pre-bend
D – bend release
H – hammer-on
P – pull-off
S – slide
tr – trill
◎ – sustained note (tie) pick only once and keep the sound going using left hand fingering
gliss – glissando. In some places the symbols / or \ are used.
~ – vibrato
harm – harmonics
x – sound is produced by tapping the string, no definite pitch is intended.

BASS

Generally, the bass parts are written in the bass clef although the treble is also used when necessary.

DRUMS

The four spaces of the staff are used as follows (starting at the top):
tom tom (G space in bass clef); snare (E space); floor tom tom (C space); and bass drum (A space).
The signs ◊ and x when used in the B space above the staff represent the cymbal and the high-hat (O – open, + – closed).
The sign ⤒ in the F space below the staff means play the high hat with your foot.

ACROSS THE UNIVERSE

Words & Music by John Lennon & Paul McCartney.

Em7
A7
D
Bm
F#m
slith-er while_ they pass they slip a-way_____ a-cross the u-ni-verse__
Pools of sor-row waves of joy are drift-ing through my o-pen mind, pos-
Em7
Gm
B
D
A7
-sess ing and ca-ress-ing me.__
Jai__ Gu-ru_____ De - va__ Om
fp

A
G
D
No - thing's gon - na change my world
No-thing's gon-na change my world
A
G
D
C
D
Bm
No-thing's gon-na change my world
No-thing's gon-na change my world
Im-ag-es of bro-ken light which
p
mf
T
A
B
5 6 7
1 2 3
3 4 5
1 2 3
1 2 3
3 4 5
1 2 3
1 2 3
2 3 4
5 5 5 5 5 5 5 5

F#m
Em7
A7
D
Bm
F#m
dance be-fore me like a mil-lion eyes, That call me on and on a - cross the u-ni-verse,
Thoughts me-an-der like a rest-less wind__ in-side a let-ter box they
Em7
A7
D
D
tum-ble blind-ly as they make their way a-cross the u-ni-verse__
Jai__ Gu-ru____ De - va__

A7
Om
No-thing's gon-na change my world
G
D
No-thing's gon-na change my world
A7
No-thing's gon-na change my world
G
D
No-thing's gon-na change my world
E
1.
D
Bm
Sounds of laugh-ter shades of earth are

Repeat & Fade Out

ACT NATURALLY

Words by Vonnie Morrison. Music by Johnny Russell.

A
G
(4x only Harmony)
C
G
(1x) They're gon-na put me in the mo - - vies
(2x,4x) hope you come and see me in the mo - - vies
(3x) make the scene a-bout a man that's sad and lo - ne - ly
they're gon-na make a big
then I know that you
and beg-gin down up-on
2x, 3x 4x
2x, 3x, 4x
2x. 3x
D7
G
star out of me
will plain - ly see
his ben - ded knee
We'll make a film a-bout a man that's sad and lo-
The big-gest fool that e-ver hit the big
I'll play the part but I won't need re-he-
2x 3x 4x
3x
2x

C
D7
G
4x only Harmony
to
- ne - ly
time
- ar - sin'
and all I got - ta do is act na - tural - ly
and all I got - ta do is act na - tural - ly
all I have to do is act na - tural - ly
1x. 4x
3x
2x 3x
4x
1. 3.
B D7
G
Well I'll bet you I'm gon - na be a big star might

D7
G
D7
win an Os - car you can't ne - ver tell the mo - vies gon - na
G
A7
make me a big star 'Cause I can play the part so well
gliss.

D7
2.
G
C D7
Well I
gliss
gliss.
G
D7

D7
G
We'll
Coda
G
D.S.
D7
G

ALL I'VE GOT TO DO

Words & Music by John Lennon & Paul McCartney.

E
C#m
F#m
All I got-ta do
Is call you on the phone and
All I got-ta do
Is whis-per in your ear the
All I got to do
Is call you on the phone and
1x Start
D.S.
2X
H.H. Open
Am
E
1.
you'll come run-ning home yeh that's all I got-ta do
And when I
words you want to hear and I'll be kiss-ing you
you'll come run-ning home yeh that's all I got-ta do
(H.H. Close)
1x only

2.
B
E
A
D.S.
C#m
And the same goes for me when-e-ver you want me at all I'll be here yes I will when-e-ver you can you
(Chorus)
Ah
Ah
just got-ta call on me yeh you just got-ta call on me
And when I
to
(H.H. Close)
D.S.

Fade Out

ALL MY LOVING

Words & Music by John Lennon & Paul McCartney.

A
F#m
D
B7
B F#m
- mem - ber I'll all - ways be true
hope that my dreams will come true
And then while I'm a - way
- mem - ber I'll all - ways be true
And then while I'm a - way
T
A
B
B
E
C#m
A
B
I'll write home ev' - ry-day And I'll send all my lov - ing to you
I'll write home ev' - ry-day And I'll send all my lov - ing to you

E
1.
2. 3.
E
C
C#m
C#mΔ7
C
I'll pre-tend
All my lov-ing
I will send to you
Woo
E
C#m
C#mΔ7
C
E
to Φ
All my lov-ing darl-ing I'll be true
Woo
D.S.x
D.S.x

E
D A
E
F#m
B7
E
Close your eyes
Close your eyes
D.S.

Coda
E
E
C#m
E
All my lov - ing
All my lov - ing
Woo
Woo
C#m
E
Woo All my lov-ing
I will send to you
Woo
Woo
T
A
B

ALL TOGETHER NOW

Words & Music by John Lennon & Paul McCartney.

𝄋 1. (Straight)
A
G
D7
One, two, three, four,
A, B, C, D.
Black, white, green, red.
Can I have a lit-tle more
Can I bring my friend to tea
Can I take my friend to bed
Five, six, seven, eight, nine, ten, I love you
E, F, G, H, I, J, I love you
Pink, Brown, yellow, orange and blue I love you
(1x Tacet)
(1x, 2x Tacet)
to ⊕ 1.
D.S x

1.
2.
𝄋2.
B
G
C
G
Bom Bom Bom
Bom - pa Bom
Sail the ship
Bom - pa Bom
D
D
G
D
1 x Tacet
C
D7
Chop the tree
Bom - pa Bom
Skip the rope
Bom - pa Bom
Look at me
D.S.2X
G
A
D.S.2X

D7
to ⊕2.
C G
All to-ge-ther now All to-ge - ther now All to-ge-ther now All to-ge - ther
A
D
now All to-ge-ther now All to-ge - ther now All to-ge-ther now All to-ge - ther now
D7
G
A
D
D.S. 1

Coda
D
G
(Lower Part 1X Tacet)
D7
All to-ge-ther now All to-ge-ther now All to-ge-ther now All to-ge-ther now All to-ge-ther now All to-ge-ther now All to-ge-ther
D
A
now All to-ge-ther now All to-ge-ther now All to-ge-ther now now Bom Bom Bom
1.
2.
Coda 2.
E
(3 times)
(Lower Part 1X 3X Tacet)
All to-ge-ther now All to-ge-ther now
(Poco Accel.)
D.S. 2.
(Hand Clap) 1X Tacet

G
D7
1.2.
G
All to-ge - ther now All to-ge-ther now All to-ge - ther now All to-ge-ther now All to-ge - ther now All to-ge-ther now
A
D
3.
D7
G
All to - ge - ther now
A
D

ALL YOU NEED IS LOVE

Words & Music by John Lennon & Paul McCartney.

Em
G
D
Em
D7
G
D
love
Love
love
love
Love
love
love
(Cello)
1. (Straight)
B
G Ah
D/F#
Em
(Chorus)
There's no-thing you can do that can't be done
There's no-thing you can make that can't be made
There's no-thing you can know that is-n't known
(Violin) 1 X Tacet

G
D/F#
Em
D7/A
G
D/F#
D/E
Ah
Ah
No-thing you can sing that can't be sung
No-one you can save that can't be saved
No-thing you can see that is-n't shown
No-thing you can say but you can learn how to play the game It's
No-thing you can do but you can learn how to be you in time It's
No-where you can be that is-n't where you're meant to be. It's
D
D/C
D/B
D
ea - sy
ea - sy
ea - sy
2.
C
G
A7
D7
(Upper Part D.S.1X, D.S.2X)
D.S.2X
All to - ge - ther
All you need is love
1x Only
D.S.2X
T
A
B
1 2 3
D.S.2X

G
A7
D7
D.S.2X
Ev-ry-bo-dy
B7
Em
Em7
D
C△7
Upper Part (D.S.1X, D.S.2X)
Middle Part (2X, D.S.1X, D.S.2X)
(D.S.2X)
All you need is love
All you need is love love
Love is all you need
1X Tacet
(Cello)
1.
D
D
F#
Love Love Love
Electric Guitar
Acoustic Guitar B 1~5 Col

D7/A
G
D/F#
D/E
D
D/C
D/B
D
2.3.
G
Love
love
love
(Acoustic Guitar)
D.S. 1. 2.
Coda
G
E
G
That is all___ you need
Love is all_______ you need
That is all___ you need
That is all___
8va
Repeat & Fade Out

AND I LOVE HER

Words & Music by John Lennon & Paul McCartney.

C#m
F#m
C#m
F#m
C#m
A
2×
__ my love___
ev'-ry-thing___
__that shine___
That's all I do
And ten-der-ly
Dark is the sky
2× D.S.×
And if you saw___ my love___
The kiss my lov-er brings___
I know this love of mine___
You'd love her too___
She brings to me___
will ne-ver die___
B7
Eb
to Φ
B
C#m
B
I___ love___ her___
And I love___ her___
And I love___ her___
A love like ours___

C#m
G#m
B
Could ne-ver die
As long as I have you near me
D.S.
Coda
C
Gm
Dm
gliss.
s

B♭
C
F
D
Gm
Bright are the stars
Dm
that shine
Gm
Dark is the sky
Dm
Gm
I know this love of mine
Dm

B♭
C7
F6
E Gm
Will ne - ver die
And I love her
Ooh
F6
Gm
D

AND YOUR BIRD CAN SING

Words & Music by John Lennon & Paul McCartney.

E
F#m
A
- thing you want And your bird can sing But you don't get me, ___ you don't get
se - ven won - ders And your bird is green But you can't see me, ___ you can't see
E
1.
2.
E
B G#m
G#mΔ7
G
me ___
me ___
When your prized ___ pos - ses - sions
When your bird ___ is bro - ken
2×

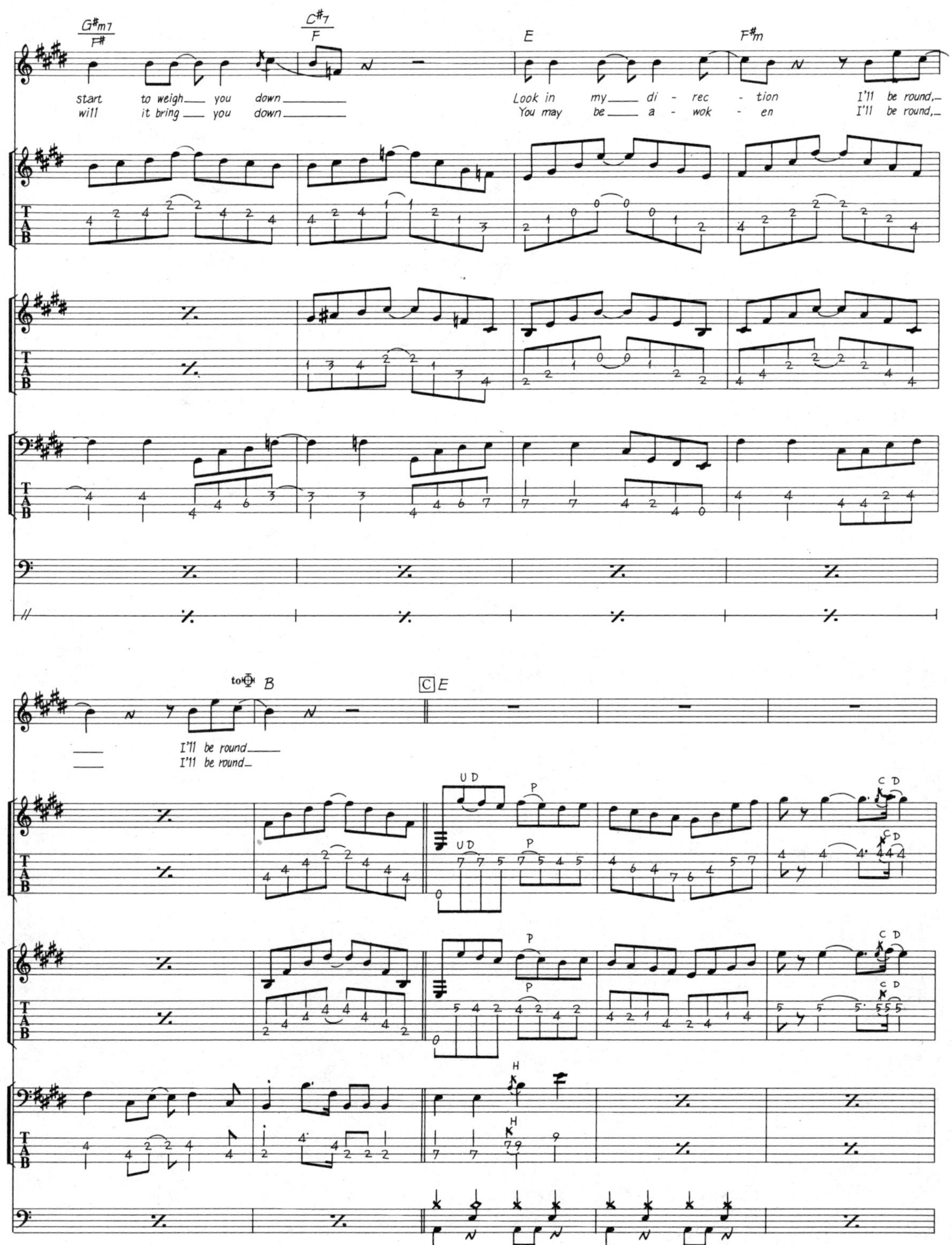
G#m7/F#
C#7/F
E
F#m
start to weigh you down
will it bring you down
Look in my di - rec - tion I'll be round,
You may be a - wok - en I'll be round,
to Φ B
C E
I'll be round
I'll be round

E
F♯m
A
E
D.S.
Coda
B
D E
You tell me that you've heard ev-ery sound there is
And your bird can

E
F#m
A
E
swing But you can't hear me,
you can't hear me
E
H
UD
P
CD

E
F#m
A
E
Tempo Rubato
A
E
Fade Out

ANNA (GO TO HIM)

Words & Music by Arthur Alexander.

Bm
D
Bm
D
Bm
D
Bm
you come and ask me girl
To set you free, girl
You say he loves you more than me___ So I will___
Em
A
D
Bm
D
Bm
set you free___ Go with him
go with him
Anna
Anna
H
T
A
B

A'
D
Bm
D
Bm
D
A - n-na girl, be-fore you go now I want you to know, now
A - n-na just one more thing, girl
Bm
D
Bm
Em
A
D
That I still love you so, But if he loves you more, go with him
You give back your ring to me And I will set you free, go with him
Ah

B
G
All of my life
I've been search-ing
for a girl
To love me
like
D
Ah
Ah
I
love
you
oh, now
But let me tell you now
B'
But
e-very girl
I
e-ver had
Ah
Ah
1 2 3

G
E
A
breaks my heart And leaves me sad, what am I what am I sup-posed to do
Ah
Ah
Ah
1.
2.
C
D
Bm
D
oh, oh, oh, oh, oh, oh, oh, oh, oh, oh, oh, oh, A - n-na just one more thing, girl

Bm
D
Bm
Em
A
D
Bm
You give back your ring to me ___ And I will set you free ___, go with him
go with
Anna
D
Bm
D
Bm
rit.
D
him
You can go with him girl
go with him
Anna
Anna
go with him

ANOTHER GIRL

Words & Music by John Lennon & Paul McCartney.

B
1. (Straight)
2. (Straight)
A
G
A
D7
A
You're ma - king me say that I've got no-bo - dy but you But as from to -
She's sweet-er than all the girls and I've met quite a few No-bo - dy in all
(D.S.1x, D.S.2x) I don't wan-na say that I've been un-hap - py with you But as from to
D.S.1x
2x
h.C
D
C
(Dubbing Bass Drum)
G
A
D7
- day well I've got some-bo - dy that's new I ain't no fool and I don't
the world can do what she can do And so I'm tell-ing you this
- day well I've seen some-bo - dy that's new I ain't no fool and I don't

D7
E7
C
A7
D7
take what I don't want, For I have got
time you'd bet-ter stop For I have got
take what I don't want, For I have got
an - oth-er girl
an - oth-er girl
Guitar II
D.S.1X
A7
to ⊕ D
D7
C
G7
C
an - oth-er girl who will love me till the end
D.S.2X
an - oth-er girl who will love me till the end
D.S.1X

G7
C
E7
A
E7
Through thick and thin she will al - ways be my friend
Through thick and thin she will al - ways be my friend
2x
8va
D.S.1X
Dubbing Bass Drum
Coda
A7
D7
A7
D.S. 1.
2.(al Coda)
an - oth-er girl
an - oth-er girl

ANY TIME AT ALL

Words & Music by John Lennon & Paul McCartney.

to
Bm
G
A7
D
D.S.x
A - ny time at
all all you've got-ta do is call And I'll be there
2x
D.S.x
3x, D.S.x
1. 2.
B
D
F#m/C#
Bm
Gm/Bb
If you need some - bo-dy to love Just look in-to my eyes
If the sun has fa-ded a-way I'll try to make it shine

D/A
A
D
F#m/C#
I'll be there to make you feel right if you're feel - ing sor- ry and sad
There is no- thing I won't do if you need a shoul- der to cry on
Bm
Gm/Bb
D/A
A
I'd real- ly sym- pa - thize Don't you be sad Just call me to - night
I hope it will be mine Call me to- night And I'll come to you

C
3.
D
A7
Bm7
A
A7
A-ny time__ at
A7
Bm7
A
A7
G
A7

G
A7
D
A-ny time at
D.S.
Coda
G
A
D
all All you've got-ta do is call And I'll be there

ASK ME WHY

Words & Music by John Lennon & Paul McCartney.

E
F#m
G#m
F#m
E
And it's true that it rea - lly on - ly goes to show
And in time, you'll un - der - stand the rea - son why
And it's true
And in time
G#7
C#m
Am
to Φ 1
That I know that I, I, I, I
If I cry it's not be - cause I'm sad
should ne - ver ne - ver ne - ver be
But you're the on - ly love that I've e - ver
ou
ou

B 𝄋 2.
1.
2.
F#
B E F#m
E
D.S.2x
Eaug
A
blue Now you're had I can't be - lie - ve
Now you're
B
E
Eaug
A
B
it's ha-ppened to me I can't con - cei - ve of a - ny - more
ha-ppend to me a - ny - more

E
E F#m C G#m
A
G#m
mi-se - ry Ask me why, I'll say I love you And I'm al - ways think - ing of
mi-se - ry Ask me why
ou
ou
A
to 2. E
E F#m
Coda 1. F#
you
I love
blue
ou
I love
D.S. 1.

B
D G#m
A
G#m
A
Ask me why, I'll say I love you And I'm al - ways think - ing of you
Ask me why
ou
ou
ou
D.S. 2
Coda 2
E
A/E
E
A/E
G#m7
you
you
ou
ou
ou
ou

BABY IT'S YOU

Words & Music by Hal David, Burt Bacharach & Barney Williams.

A
C
G
C
It's not the way you smile that touched my heart
You should hear what they say a - bout you cheat cheat
It's not the way you kiss
They say they say you ne-ver
la
Sha la la la la la
G
Em
B
that tears me apart
ne-ver e-ver been true
But how (1.) ma-ny ma-ny ma-ny nights go by
Wo ho (2.3.) it does-n't ma-tter what they say
2x
(cheat cheat) ou

Am
G
Em
C
I sit a-lone a-t home and cry o-ver you
What can I do
Can't help my-
I know I'm gon-na love you any old way What can I do
then it's true
Don't want no-
Ou
Ah
D
G
Em
G
to
1.
Em
-self
Cause ba-by it's you
Ba-by it's you
-bo-dy no-bo-dy
Cause ba-by it's you
Ba-by it's you
Sha la la la la la la
Sha la la la la la la
Sha la la la

2.
C
Em
C
D
G
C
la
D
G
Coda
Em
G
Wo ho
Don't leave me all a - lone
la
Sha la la la la la
D.S.
Fade Out

BABY'S IN BLACK

Words & Music by John Lennon & Paul McCartney.

A D A E B A A7 D
oh___, what can I___ do?
She___ thinks of him and so she dress-es in black. And
I___ think of her but she thinks on-ly of him. And
2x
(8va Low)
A E A
though he'll nev-er come back, she's dressed in black
though it's on-ly a whim, she thinks of him
𝄋 1.
C F#m B7 D
Oh, how long will it___ take till she

E
D A
E
D
E
A
D
to 2.
sees the mis-take she has made? Dear, what can I __ do?
(oh,)
D.S.2x
Ba-by's in __ black and I'm __ feel-ing blue. Tell me oh ___, what can I __
A
E
to 1. E A
E
D
E
A
do?
(8va Low)

A
Coda 1
A
A7
D
She thinks of him and so she dress-es in black And
(Rim)
D.S. 1 al Coda 1
A E A E
though he'll ne-ver come back she's dressed in black
Coda 2
A E A
do ?
D.S. 2 al Coda 2

BABY YOU'RE A RICH MAN

Words & Music by John Lennon & Paul McCartney.

G7
C/G
G7
C
(Straight)
A
G
1x D.S.x C (G)
(1x) How does it feel___ to be one of the beau - ti - ful
(2x) How does it feel___ to be one of the beau - ti - ful
(D.S.x) How does it feel___ to be one of the beau - ti - ful
1x only
2x
D.S.x
2x D.S.x
(S.D.)

G7
2x D.S.x
Fadd9
G
G
F
G
peo-ple
peo-ple
peo-ple
Now that you know who you are
How of-ten have you been there
Tuned to a na - tu-ral E
what do you want to be
of-ten e-nough to know
hap-py to be that way
2x
T
A
B
C
G
G
F
G
And have you tra - velled ve-ry far
What did you see when you were there
Now that you've found an-oth-er key
2x Elec. Piano
Tambourine

1.
2.
B
F
G
C
C
G
far as the eye can see
no-thing that does - n't show
what are you go-ing to play
(1X D.S.X) Ba - by you're a rich man
E.Pf
E.Pf
C
G
D.S.x
C
Ba - by you're a rich man
Ba - by, you're a rich man
too
You

B♭6
G7/B
C
G7
C
D.S.x
Ba - by
keep all your mo-ney in a big brown bag in-side a zoo
what a thing to do
G
C
G
to Φ
Ba - by you're a rich man Ba - by you're a rich man Ba - by you're a rich man

Coda
C
too
D.S.
C
too oh
C
G
Ba - by you're a rich man
C
Ba - by
Ba - by you're a rich man
G
Ba - by you're a rich man
C
too wah wah
Repeat & Fade Out

BACK IN THE USSR

Words & Music by John Lennon & Paul McCartney.

A
A D C D
(1.) Flew in fr - om Mia - mi Beach B - O - A - C Didn't get to bed last night On
(2.) Been a - way so long I hard - ly knew the place Gee it's good to be back home Leave
(D.S.) me round your snow peaked moun - tain way down south Take me to your dad - dy's farm Let
(Jet)
(Acoustic Piano)
8va
(Hand Clap)
A D C D
the way the pa - per bag was on my knee Man I had a dread - ful flight I'm back in the U. S. S. R.
it till to - mor - row to un - pack my case Ho - ney dis - con - nect the phone I'm back in the U. S. S. R.
me hear your ba - la - lai - ka's ring - ing out Come and keep your com - rade warm I'm back in the U. S. S. R.
2x Tom
2x Snare

A
C
D
to
You don't know how luc - ky you are boy
You don't know how luc - ky you are boy
You don't know how luc - ky you are boy
D.S.X
Hey
(Guitar I)
(Guitar III)
2X
D.S.X
(Hand Clap)
1.
D
A
B7
E7
2.
N.C.
Back in the U. S. S. R.
Yeah
Back in the U. S. Back in the U. S. Back in the
8va

B
D7
N.C.
A
A7
Upper Part Chorus
Lower Part Chorus
wu
U. S. S. R.
dan dan dan dan dan dan dan dan dan dan
Well the U - kraine girls real - ly knock me out They
A
A7
D
D/C#
D/C
B7
E7
dan dan dan dan dan dan dan dan dan dan dan dan dan dan dan dan
leave the west be-hind And Mos - cow girls make me sing and shout That Geor-gia's al-ways on my my my
2X
Tom
H.H. Poco Open

D7
1.
A
B7
E7
C
A
D
dan dan dan dan
my my my my my my mind
oh Come on
Hu Hey
2x
8va
(Hand Clap)
C
D
A
D
C
Hu Hey
AH Yeah
Yeah Yeah
Yeah

D
D
A
C
D
I'm back in the U. S. S. R.
You don't know how luc - ky you are
boys
h.c
(Guitar III)
A
A7
2.
A
B7
E7
Back in the U. S. S. R.
Lower Part Chorus
dan dan dan
Well the
mind
oh
show
gliss.

D.S.

Coda
D
A
B7
E7
E
A
Back in the U. S. S. R.
oh
let me tell you ho-ney
(Shouting)
gliss.
8va
(Guitar III)
H
(Hand Clap)
wu
wu

BAD BOY

Words & Music by Larry Williams.

A
C7
bad lit-tle kid moved in to my neigh-bor-hood,
Buys ev-'ry rock and roll book on the mag-a-zine stand
Gon-na tell ya mam-ma, you'd bet-ter do what she said;
He won't do noth-in' right, just a
Ev-'ry dime that he gets, oh he's
Get to the bar-ber shop and get that
D.S.x only
sit-tin' got to look so good.
off to the juke-box man.
hair cut off your head.
F7
He don't wan-na go to school and learn to read and write,
Well he wor-ries that teach-er till at night she's a-read-y to poop,
You shoot the can-ar-y and you fed it to the neigh-bor's cat,

F7
Just sits a-round the house and plays that rock and roll mu-sic all night.
From rock-in' and a roll-in', spin-nin' in a hu-la-hoop.
You gave the cock-er span-iel a bath in moth-er's laun-dro-mat.
G7
F7
Well he put thumb tacks on teach-er's chair, put chew'n gum in li'l girl's hair.
Well his rock and roll has got-ta stop, Jun-ior's head is hard as rock.
Well ya mam-ma said it's got-ta stop. Jun-ior's head is hard as rock.
HU D
C
QC

to
1.
2.
B
C7
G7
G7
C7
Now, Jun - ior be - have your-self!
-have your-self! Ow!
D.S. x
Ow!
C
U D
C
HU D
S
H P

F7
C7
G7
Ow!
F7
C7
G7
D.S.
Coda
C7
have your-self! Ooo!

THE BALLAD OF JOHN AND YOKO

Words & Music by John Lennon & Paul McCartney.

E
E7
trying to get to Hol - land or France
hon - ey - moon - ing down by the Seine
talk - ing in our beds for a week
eat - ing choc' - late cake in a bag
fif - ty a - corns tied in a sack
The man in the mac said you've
Pe - ter Brown called to say you can
The news - pa - pers said say what're you
The news - pa - pers said she's
The men from the press said we
UD
12
got to go back you know they did - n't ev - en give us a chance
make it O. K. you can get mar - ried in Gib - ral - ter near Spain
do - ing in bed I said we're on - ly trying to get us some peace
gone to his head they look just like two Gu - rus in drag
wish you suc - cess it's good to have the both of you back
Christ! You know it ain't ea -
2x
D.S. repeat x
D.S.x
1 2 3
T
A
B

A
E
(Upper Part D.S.time & D.S.repeat time)
- sy
you know how hard it can be
The way things are go -
D.S. repeat time
2x
B7
to
1.2.4.
E
3.
E
- ing
they're going to cru - ci - fy
me
Drove from
gliss

E
B
A
Sav-ing up your mo-ney for a rai - ny day
giv-ing all your clothes to cha - ri - ty
Last night the wife said Oh boy when you're dead you don't take no-thing with you but your soul think!
D.S.

Coda
C
E
B7
E
B7
E
E6
me
The way things are go - ing
they're going to cru - ci - fy
me
(Maracas)

BECAUSE

Words & Music by John Lennon & Paul McCartney.

A7
A7(13)
D
Ddim
A
C#m
Ah
Be - cause the world is
- cause the wind is
- cause the sky is
D#m7-5
G#7
A
C#m
round, it turns me on:
high, it blows my mind;
blue, it makes me cry;
Be - cause the world is
Be - cause the wind is
Be - cause the sky is

A7
A7(13)
to Φ
1.
D
Ddim
2.
D
round.
high.
blue.
Ah
Be -
Ah
P
T
A
B
Ddim
B F#
G#7
Love is old, love is new;
Love is all, love is you.
Be -
(Brass.)
8va. bassa
D.S.

Coda
D
Ddim
C
C#m
D#m7-5
G#7
Ah
(Synth)
A
C#m
A7
A7(13)
D
Ddim
T
A
B

BEING FOR THE BENEFIT OF MR. KITE

Words & Music by John Lennon & Paul McCartney.

Bb Dm G Cm Gaug
there will be a show to-night on tram-po-line The Hen-der-sons will all be there
-forms his feat on Sat-ur-day at Bish-ops-gate The Hen-der-sons will dance and sing as
Mis-ter K. per-forms his tricks with-out a sound And Mis-ter H. will dem-on-strate ten
T A B
Bb Dm A Dm Dm7 Bb A
late of Pab-lo Fan-ques' fair what a scene O-ver men and hor-ses hoops and gar-ters last-ly through a hogs head of
Mis-ter Kite flies through the ring don't be late Mes-s'rs K. and H. as-sure the pub-lic their pro-duc-tion will be se-cond to
som-er-sets he'll un-der-take on so-lid-ground Hav-ing been some days in prep-a-ra-tion, a splen-did time is guar-an-teed for
Rim.

Dm
to
1.
Gm
A
Dm
Gm
A
Dm
real__ fire__
none
all
In this way
And of
And to
Mis - ter K. will chal-lange the world
The
2x
2.
Gm
A
B Dm
DmΔ7
Dm7
Dm6
A
course
Hen - ry the horse
danc - es the
waltz.
S. E.
8va

A
Dm
DmΔ7
Dm7
Dm6
B
Em
(Synth)
8va
C
B
Em
C
B
Em
G
The
S.E.
8va
D.S.

Coda
Gm
A
Dm
Gm
A
C Dm
DmΔ7
Dm7
Dm6
night Mis - ter Kite is top-ping the bill
S.E.
T
A
B
A
Dm
DmΔ7
Dm7
Dm6
B

Em
C
B
Em
C
B
Em
C
B
Em
C
B
Em
Fill

BIRTHDAY

Words & Music by John Lennon & Paul McCartney.

D7
A7
E7
h.c
A7
A
A7
You say it's your birth- day
It's my birth-day too Yeah
D.S. 2x Hand Clap.
D.S. 2x Tambourine

D7
They say it's your birth - day
A7
We're gon-na have a good time
E7
I'm
h.c
D.S.2x
glad it's your birth - day
to ⊕ 2. A7
Hap-py birth - day to __ you
B N.C.
Tambourine

N.C.
C E
H. Clap
Tambourine
Yes we're go-in' to a par - ty par - ty
Yes we're go-in' to a par - ty par - ty
Yes we're go-in' to a par - ty par - ty

D
C
G
I would like you to dance
(birth - day) Take a cha-cha-cha-chance
(Birth - day) I would
(Organ)
(Piano)
D.S.1x
No Crash
like you to dance
(Birth - day) Ooo
dance!
to ⊕ 1.
E
B
Yeah
2.
N.C.
8va
W.C
U D
D.S.1x

92

N.C.
Coda 1. E/B
E
8va
w.c
c D
H P
Tambourine
D.S. 1.
D.S. 2.
Coda 2.
A7
Hap-py birth - day to — you
(Slow)
h.c
S

BLACKBIRD

Words & Music by John Lennon & Paul McCartney.

Em
EmΔ7
E♭
D
A7
C♯
C
Cm
G
B
A7
D7
G
to Φ
All your life
You were on - ly wait - ing for this mo - ment to a - rise
All your life
You were on - ly wait - ing for this mo - ment to be free
Bird Singing
1.
C
G
B
A7
D7
G
B
2.
F
C
E
Dm
C
B♭
C
F
C
E
Dm
C
Black - bird fly
Black - bird fly

C
B♭6
A7
D7
G
Am7
G/B
G
1.
C
A7/C#
D
B7/D#
In - to the light of the dark black night
gliss.
2×( )
Em
EmΔ7/E♭
D
A7/C#
C
Cm
G/B
A7
D7
G

2.
G
rit.
G Am7 G/B C G/B A7 D7
gliss.
gliss
Bird Singing
D.S.
Coda
C G/B A7 D7 G C G/B A7 D7 G
You were on-ly wait-ing for this mo - ment to a-rise
You were on-ly wait-ing for this mo - ment to a-rise
Bird Singing

BLUE JAY WAY

Words & Music by George Harrison.

A (3times)
C
Cdim
C
Cdim
C
There's a fog up on L. (1x) A.
(2x) show
(3x) know
And my friends have lost their way
And I told them where to go
And I'd real-ly like to go
(Chorus)
(1x, 2x Tacet)
Know
go
(1x Tacet)
3x 8va lower
Dubbing Tape Reverse
1x
(2x, 3x)
Cdim
C(b5)
Cdim
C
B
1. 2.
C6
CΔ7
We'll be o ver soon they said
Ask a p'lice-man on the street
Soon will be the break of day
Now they've lost them-selves in-stead
There's so ma-ny there to meet
Sit-ting here in Blue Jay Way
Please don't
(Fast)
day
way
(Top)

C
CΔ7
CΔ7
C6
CΔ7
CΔ9
C
CΔ7
CΔ7
C6
CΔ7
C
CΔ7
CΔ7
C6
be long
Please don't you be ve - ry long
Please don't be long
or
(1X Tacet)
Don't be long
Don't be long
2X
2X
C
CΔ7
C6
C
C(b5)
C
Slower
Cdim
3.
(4 times)
C6
CΔ7
C
CΔ7
I may be a - sleep
(1x) Well it on - ly goes to
(2x) Now it's past my bed I
Please don't be long
Please don't be long
Don't be
1X Tacet
2X
(Top)

1. 2. 3.
CΔ7 C6 CΔ7 CΔ9 C CΔ7 C6 CΔ7 C6 C CΔ7 C6 C
2x. 3x tacet
please don't you be ve-ry long please don't be long or I may be a-
please don't you be ve-ry long please don't be long
2x 3x
long Don't be long
1x tacet
3x 8va. lower
T A B
C(b5) C
4.
C6 CΔ7
D C
- sleep please don't be-long Don't be long don't be
please don't be-long

C
long
Don't be-long Don't be long
Don't be-long
Don't be long
Don't be long
8va

BOYS

Words & Music by Luther Dixon & Wes Farrell.

A 𝄋 (Straight)
E7
(1.) I've been told when a boy kiss a girl
Take a trip a - round the world Hey
(2.3.) My girl says when I kiss her lips
Get the thrill thru fin - ger tips Hey
D.S.X
A7
Hey
Hey
E7
Hey
Hey
bop shoo-wa
bop bop shoo- wa
bop shoo-wa
bop bop shoo - wa

B7
A7
E7
B7
Hey
Yes they say you do
Yeah she said you do
Well I talk a-bout
bop shoo-wa
bop bop shoo-wa
bop shoo-wa
B
E7
A7
boys
Don't you know I mean boys
Well I talk a-bout boys now
Yeah yeah boys
Yeah yeah boys
Yeah yeah boys

A7
E7
B7
A7
Ah
boys
Well I talk a-bout boys now
What a bun-dle of joy
Yeah yeah boys
Yeah yeah boys
E7
1x only
to Φ
B7
C
E7
(All-right George)
yeah, yeah

E7
A7
E7
B7
A7
E7
B7
8va
T
A
B
D.S.

Coda
B7
E7
A7
Ah, Yeah! boys
Don't you know I mean boys
Oh
Yeah, yeah boys
boys
Ah
Ah
Well I talk a - bout
Fade Out

CAN'T BUY ME LOVE

Words & Music by John Lennon & Paul McCartney.

G6
B
C7
2x
D.S.1x
D.S.2x
I'll buy you a dia - mond ring my friend if it makes you feel al - right I'll
(2x) give you all I've got to give if you say you love me too I
(D.S.1x D.S.2x) you don't need no dia-mond ring And I'll be sa-tis - fied Tell
(H.H. OPEN)
F7
C7
G7
get you a - ny - thing my friend if it makes you feel al - right 'Cause I don't care too
may not have a lot to give but what I've got I'll give to you For I don't care too
me that you want those kind of things that mo-ney just can't buy For I don't care too

F7
C7
C7
C
Em
much for mo-ney for mo-ney Can't buy me love
much for mo-ney for mo-ney Can't buy me love
much for mo-ney for mo-ney Can't buy me love
I'll Can't buy me love
D.S.2x
(H.H.Closed.)
(H.H.OPen)
Am
C7
Em
Am
Ev' - ry - bo - dy tells me so Can't buy me love

Coda 1.
Dm7
G6
C7
D C7
No no no no Say Ah
D.S. 1.
F7
C7
Guitar II
Guitar III

C7
G7
F7
C7
E
Em
Can't buy me love
Am
C7
Em
Am
Ev' - ry-bo-dy tell me so
Can't buy me love

Dm7
G6
No no no no Say
Coda 2.
C7
F
Em
Am
Ooh Can't buy me love love
D.S. 2.
Em
Am
Dm7
G6
C7
Can't buy me love no

CARRY THAT WEIGHT

Words & Music by John Lennon & Paul McCartney.

C
C
G7
to
time
Boy,
you're gon - na
Car - ry That Weight
Car - ry That Weight
a - long
C
C/B
B
Am7
Am7/D
Dm7
G7
time.
(Brass)
S
H

C△7
C
F△7
Bm7-5
E7
Am7
(Brass.)
(E.Guitar)
hu D
P
S
h.c
H
D
Am7
Am7/D
Dm7
G7
C△7
I ne-ver give you my pil - low,
I on-ly send you my in - vi - ta - tion
8va

F△7
Bm7-5
E7
Am7
G7
And in the mid-dle of the cel - e-bra - tions, I break down.
(Brass)
D.S.
Coda
C
G/B
A
C
G/B
A
time.
(E.Guitar)

CHAINS

Words & Music by Gerry Goffin & Carole King.

B♭
E♭9
ba - by's got me locked up in chains___ And they ain't the kind that you can
I can't break a - way from there chains___ Can't___ run a - round 'cause I'm not
5 6 7
B♭
F9
E♭9
B♭
see ___ Woh___ it's chains of___ love ___ got a hold on me___, yeah___
free ___ Woh___ these chains of___ love ___ won't___ let me be___, yeah___
6 7 8
7 8 9
5 6 7
6 7 8

1.
2.
F
B♭7
to Φ
B
E♭9
B♭
pa - lum-pa - lum-pa - lum-pa
I wan - na tell you pre - tty ba - by
please be - lieve we when I tell you
I think you're
your lips are
B♭7
E♭9
F
fine
sweet
I'd like to love you
I'd like to kiss them
But, dar - ling, I'm im - pri - soned by these
But, I can't break a - way from all these
D.S. 1. 2.

Coda
B♭
Chains, chains of love chains of
love chains of love
E♭
E♭m
Fade Out

COME TOGETHER

Words & Music by John Lennon & Paul McCartney.

D7+9
A
G7
jew, jew, eyeballs He want ho - ly rol-lers He got hair down to his knees
Got to be a jok-er He just do what he please
B D7+9
shoo
shoo
shoo
shoo
C D7+9
He wear no shoe shine He got
He Bag Pro-duc-tion, He got
He rol-ler coas-ter He got
Stick

D7+9
A
toe jam foot-ball He got mon - key fin-ger He shoot Co - ca Co - la He say, "I know_ you, you know_ me
wal - rus gum-boot He got O - no side-board He one spi - nal crack - er He got feet down be-low_ his knees
ear - ly warn-ing He got mud - dy wa-ter He one Mo - jo fil-ter He say, one, and one, and one_ is three
G7
Bm
A
to Φ
1.
2.
G
A
G
A
One thing I can tell you is You got to be free_"
Hold you in his arm chair, You can feel his dis-ease_
Got to be good look-ing cause, He's so hard to see_
Come to - geth - er
Right now_ o - ver me now_ o - ver me

D7+9
shoo
Right
D D7+9
He come
A
8va
8va

D7+9
Coda
G
A7
E D7+9
now
o-ver me
8va
D.S.
Stick
HH
F D7+9
shoo
shoo
shoo
oh
Come to-ge-ther,
T.C

D7+9
yeah
Come to-ge - ther,
yeah
Come to-ge - ther,
yeah
Come to-ge - ther,
yeah
Come to-ge - ther,
yeah
Come to-ge - ther
yeah_

D7+9
Come to-ge - ther, yeah
Ah
Come to-ge - ther yeah
Come to-ge - ther yeah
Come to-ge - ther
Fade Out

THE CONTINUING STORY OF BUNGALOW BILL

Words & Music by John Lennon & Paul McCartney.

C
Fm
C
Fm
G
A
E
A
Dm
what did you kill
Bun-ga-low Bill
Hey
Bun-ga-low Bill
What did you kill
2x tacet
A
Dm
E
(Slow down)
B Am
C
F
F
G
Bun-ga-low Bill
(1x) He went out ti-ger hun-ting with his e-le-phant and gun
(2x) Deep in the jun-gle where the migh-ty ti-ger lies
(3x) The child-ren asked him if to kill was not a sin
(with tremolo)
3x
1x only

Am C F G E G Am Fm
In case of ac - ci-dents he al-ways took his mom He's the all Ameri-can bul-let-head-ed sax-on mother's son
Bill and his e-le-phants were ta-ken by sur-prise So Cap-tain Mar-vel zapped him right bet-ween the eyes zA
"Not when he looked so fierce." his mom-my but-ted in If looks could kill it would have been us in-stead of him
8va.
Guitar III
Guitar II
a tempo
N.C.
All the child-ren sing
(3x only organ)
C (4 times repeat)
C G C Fm C Fm G
Hey Bun-ga-low Bill What did you kill Bun-ga-low Bill
mouth whistle 4x in
(Organ)
2x 3x 4x

A
E
A
Dm
A
Dm
E
D
N.C.
(Free)
Hey
Bun-ga-low Bill
What did you kill
Bun-ga-low Bill
4x
3x
4x
2x
Drs
(Hand Clap)
Hey Yo!
(H.Clap)

CRY BABY CRY

Words & Music by John Lennon & Paul McCartney.

B
Em
EmΔ7
Em7
Em6
C7
G
King of Mar - i - gold was in the kitch - en cooking break - fast for the queen The
King was in the gar - den pick - ing flow - ers for a friend who came to play The
Duch - ess of Kir - cal - dy al - ways smil - ing and ar - riv - ing late for tea The
Twelve o'clock a meet - ing 'round the ta - ble for a se - ance in the dark With
1x only
1x tacet
E.Gt. 3x only
1x tacet
1x tacet
queen was in the par - lor play - ing pia - no for the child - ren of the king.
queen was in the play - room paint - ing pic - tures for the child - ren's hol - i - day.
duke was hav - ing prob - lems with a mes - sage at the lo - cal Bird and Bee.
voic - es out of no - where put on spec - ially by the child - ren for a lark.
E.Gt. 3x only
1x tacet

C
G
Am
F
G
Em
A7
Cry ba - by cry
Make your mo-ther sigh
She's old e-nough to know bet-ter so
3x only (chorus)
1x tacet
She's old e-nough to know bet-ter so
8va bassa
1.2.3.
4.
cry ba - by cry
The
The
At
Cry ba - by cry cry cry cry ba-by
Make your mo-ther sigh
She's
cry ba - by cry
cry ba - by cry
She's
8va bassa
1x only

Em
A7
F
G
Am
old e-nough to know bet-ter So cry ba - by cry cry cry cry
old e-nough to know bet-ter So cry ba - by cry
F
G
Em
A7
F
Em
Make your mo-ther sigh She's old e-nough to know bet-ter So cry ba - by cry
She's old e-nough to know bet-ter So cry ba - by cry

A DAY IN THE LIFE

Words & Music by John Lennon & Paul McCartney.

Em
Em7
C
C△7
Am9
G
Bm
boy
A-bout a luck-y man who made the grade
And though the news was ra-ther
sad
Well, I just had to laugh
I saw the pho-to-graph
F
T
A
B

B
G
Bm
Em
Em7
C
CΔ7
Am9
He blew his mind out in a car
He did-n't no-tice that the lights had changed
A crowd of peo-ple stood and
stared
F
They'd seen his face be-fore
No-bo-dy was real-ly sure if he was from the House of Lords
T
A
B

C
G Bm Em Em7 C C△7 Am9 G Bm
I saw a film_ to-day_ oh_ boy
The Eng-lish arm-y had just won the war
A crowd_ of peo-ple turned a-way_
Em Em7 C F Em Em7 C C N.C.
But I_ just had to look_
Hav-ing read the book
I'd love to turn_

you on
Up and cresc.
E
Cym. Fill

D
E
E
E
D
D
Woke up
got out of bed
Dragged a comb
a-cross my head
Found my
E
B9
E
B9
B
E
E
way down stairs and drank a cup
And look-ing up
I no-ticed I was late
Ha, ha, ha, Found my
coat
and grabbed my hat
Made the

E
D
E
B9
E
B9
bus in se-conds flat
Found my way up - stairs and had a smoke And some-bo-dy spoke_ and I went in-to a dream_
F
C
G
D
A
E
C
Ah
Ah
Ah
Ah
cresc.

G
D
A
E
G
G
Bm
Ah
I read the news_ to-day_ oh
ff
Em
Em7
C
C△7
Am9
G
Bm7
boy
Four thou-sand holes_ in Black-burn Lan-ca-shire
And though the holes_ were ra - ther

Em
Em7
C
C△7
Em
Em7
small
They had to count— them all—
Now they know how ma-ny holes it takes to fill the Al - bert Hall—
C
C
N.C.
I'd love to turn you on
Up and cresc.

T
A
B
E
fff

DAY TRIPPER

Words & Music by John Lennon & Paul McCartney.

E7
(with Tambourine)
A
E7
(1.) Got a good rea - son for tak-ing the ea - sy way out.
(2.) She's a big tea - ser She took me half the way there.
(3.) Tried to please her She on - ly played one night stands.

A7
E7
Got a good rea - son for tak - ing the ea - sy way out now. She was a
She's a big tea - ser, She took me half the way there now. She was a
Tried to please her, She on - ly played one night stands, now. She was a
B
F#7
A7
Day Trip - per, One way tic - ket, Yeah.
Day Trip - per, One way tic - ket, Yeah.
Day Trip - per, Sun - day driv - er Yeah.
It took me so

to ⊕
1.
G#7
C#7
B7
E7
long to find out, and I found out.
(Tambourine)
2.
C
B7
B7
out.

B7
Ah
HUD
C
Ah
Ah
Ah
Ah
Ah
C
HUD
C
UD

E7
(Tambourine)
D.S.
Coda
B7
E7
out.

E7
(Tambourine)
E
E7
Day Trip - per,
Day Trip - per Yeah,
Repeat & Fade Out

DEAR PRUDENCE

Words & Music by John Lennon & Paul McCartney.

A
Dear Prudence
Prudence
Prudence
won't you come out to play
open up your eyes
let me see your smile
(1X, 2X Tacet)
(Guitar III)
2X D.S.X
Hand Clap (1X Tacet)
Tambourine
D.S.X
Dear Prudence
Dear Prudence
Dear Prudence
greet the brand new day
See the sunny skies
like a little child
The
The
The
(Chorus) 1X Tacet
Ah
1X Tacet
D.S.X

B
D
D C
D B
D B♭
sun is up the sky is blue It's beau - ti-ful and so are you Dear Pru - dence
wind is low the birds will sing that you are part of ev' - ry-thing Dear Pru - dence
clouds will be a dai - sy chain So let me see you smile a-gain Dear Pru - dence
Hand Clap
C
G
to Φ
1. D
2. D
G D
won't you come out to play
won't you o - pen up your
won't you let me see you
Dear eyes?
(2x) Ah
(D.S.x) Ooo
(Guitar III)
H.H. Open

C
Look a - round round
Look a-round round round
round round round round round
round round round round round
round round round round round
round round round round round
look a - round
Ah
Dear
h.c
P
D.S.

Coda
D
smile ?
Dear
Pru - dence
(Guitar IV)
(Guitar III 8va bassa)
(Hand Clap)
(Tambourine)
won't you come out to play
Dear
(Acoustic Piano)
8va

D
D/C
D/B
D/Bb
Pru - dence
greet the brand new day
The
gliss.
E
sun is up
the sky
is blue
It's beau - ti - ful
and so are you
Dear
(Chorus)
8va
1 2 3

D
D7
C
G
D
Prudence
won't you come out to play?
F
Dadd9
C/D
G/D
A/D
Fade Out

DEVIL IN HER HEART

Words & Music by Richard B. Drapkin.

(4 times repeat)
A
Am7
D7
G
(1.) heart
(2) heart no no this I can't be-lieve
(3) heart oh no no no this I can't be-lieve
(4) heart oh no no no no this I can't be-lieve
But her eyes they tan-ti-lize
(1.) She's gon-na tear your heart a-
(2.3.4.) She's gon-na tear your heart a-
(1.2.3.4.) heart
She's got a tear your heart a-
-part
oh her lips are real-ly thril-ing
no no nay will she de-cieve
1.2.3.
G7

B
C
Cm
G
G7
(1.) I'll take my chan - ces for ro-man - ce is So im - por - tant to me
(2.) I can't be - lie - ve that she'll e - ver e - ver go Not when she hu - gs and says she loves me so
(3.) Don't take chan - ces if your ro - man - ce is So im - por - tant to you
Ah
(3.) Don't take chan - ces if your ro - man - ce is So im - por - tant to you
C
Cm
A7
D7
She'll ne - ver hurt me she won't de - sert me she's an an - gel sent to me
She'll ne - ver hurt me she won't de - sert me lis - ten can't you see
She'll ne - ver hurt me she won't de - sert me she's an an - gel sent to me
Ah
(1.3.) she's an an - gel sent to me
(2.) lis - ten can't you see

4.
D7
G
C
Am7
D7
G
she's got the de-vil in her
she's got the de-vil in her
She's got the de-vil in her
she's got the de-vil in her heart
No she's an an-gel sent to me
she's got the de-vil in her
she's got the de-vil in her heart
Am7
D7
G
G6 9
She's got the de-vil in her heart
No she's an an-gel sent to me
she's got the de-vil in her heart

DIG A PONY

Words & Music by John Lennon & Paul McCartney.

D
A
F#m
Bm
(5.) I hi hi hi hi hi
(6.) I hi hi hi hi hi
(1.) I hi hi hi hi hi
(2.) I hi hi hi hi hi
(3.) I hi hi hi hi hi
(4.) I hi hi hi hi hi
1x, 3x Tacet
(2.4.5.6.) I hi hi hi hi hi
1x omit
hi
hi
feel the wind blow
cold and lone - ly
Well you can in - di - cate ev - 'ry - thing you
Well you can syn - di - cate a - ny boat you
hi
hi
hi
hi
Dig a po - ny
Do a road - hog
Pick a moon - dog
Roll a ston - - ey
Well you can cel - e - brate a - ny - thing you
Well you can pen - e trate a - ny place you
Well you can ra - di - ate ev - 'ry - thing you
Well you can im - i - tate ev - 'ry - one you
hi

G7
G
Bm
G7
see
row.
Yes,
Yes,
You can in-di-cate ev-'ry-thing
You can syn-di-cate a-ny boat
you see
you row
1.
E
want
go
are
know
Yes,
Yes,
Yes,
Yes,
you can cel-e-brate a-ny-thing
you can pen-e-trate a-ny place
You can ra-di-ate ev-ery-thing
You can im-i-tate ev-'ry-one
you want
you go
you are
you know
Ooh
Ooh
repeat time
repeat time
repeat time only
2.
E
B
G
D
A
I told you so
All I want is you
I told you so
All I want is you

to ⊕ 1. 2.
G
D
A
rit. - - -
a tempo
Ev - 'ry-thing has got to be just like you want it to
Be - cause
Ev - 'ry-thing has got to be just like you want it to
Be - cause
D.S. 1.
⊕ Coda 1.
C
A
Oh
Oh

F#m
Bm
G7
1h.C
1h.U
1h.U D
C
D
H
Bm
G
E7
S
D.S. 2.

Coda 2.
G
D
A
G
D
A
H&P
P
4.

DIG IT

Words & Music by John Lennon, Paul McCartney, George Harrison & Richard Starkey.

B♭
C
B♭
F
B♭
C
I like a Roll - ing Stone
Like the
4.
B♭
F
B♭
C
B♭
F
F. B. I.
and the C. I. A.
T
A
B

B♭
C
B♭
F
B♭
C
and the B. B. C.
4.
4.
4.
4.
4.
B♭
F
B♭
C
4
B♭
F
B. B. King
and Do - ris Day
4.
4.
8 8 8 8
8 8 8 8
8 8 8 8
10 10 10 10 10 10
8 8 8 8
8 8 8 8

B♭
C
B♭
F
B♭
C
Matt Bus - by Dig it Dig it Dig it
B♭
F
B♭
C
B♭
F
Dig it Dig it Dig it Dig it Dig it Dig it Dig it Dig it Dig it Dig it Dig it
Fade Out

DIZZY MISS LIZZY

Words & Music by Larry Williams.

D
A
E7
Ah!
Ooo
Hu
Ah
gliss.
You make me diz - zy Mi - ss Liz - zy
You make me diz - zy Mi - ss Liz - zy
Run and tell your ma - ma

A
D
The way you rock and roll
When you call my name
I want you be my bride
You make me diz - zy Mi - ss Liz - zy
Ooo ba - by
Run and tell your bro - ther
2x
h.c
U
D
D.S.x
A
E7
When we do the stroll
Say you're driv - ing me in - sane
Ba - by don't run and hide
Come on Miss Liz - zy
Come on come on come on come on ba - by
You make me diz - zy Mi - ss Liz - zy
I
Girl

D
A
1. 3.
E7
B
A
Love me 'fore I grow too old
want to be your lov-ing man
I want to mar-ry you
Come on give me fe - ver
Come on give me fe - ver
put your lit-tle hand in mine
put your lit-tle hand in mine Girl
You make me diz-zy diz-zy Liz - zy
You make me diz zy diz-zy Liz-zy
oh! Girl you look so
Girl you look so fine
gliss.

A
E7
D
to
A
fine
Just a rock-ing and a roll - ing
you're just a rock-ing and a roll - ing
Girl I said I wish you were mine
Ooo I said I wish you were mine
D.S.x(
E7
2.
Ah
Ah
Coda
A
A6
D.S.

DOCTOR ROBERT

Words & Music by John Lennon & Paul McCartney.

A7
1x
— you'd call — Doc - tor Ro-bert
— you up — Doc - tor Ro-bert
Na-tional Health, — Doc - tor Ro-bert
Day or night — he'll be there a - ny time at all —
Take a drink — from his spe-cial cup — Doc - tor
Don't pay money — just to see your-self — Doc - tor
H P
H
Doc - tor Ro-bert
Ro-bert
Ro-bert
Doc - tor Ro-bert
Doc - tor Ro-bert
Doc - tor Ro-bert
F#7
(1.3.) You're a new — and bet-ter man —
(2.) He's a man — you must be - lieve —

F#7
E7
F#7
He helps you ___ to un-der-stand ___ He does eve - ry-thing he can (1x Doc-tor)
___ Help-ing a - ny-one in need ___ No one can suc - ceed like Doc-tor Ro-
1.
B7
Ro-bert
2. 3.
B
- bert
B B
Well, ___ well, ___ well, ___ you're ___

E/B
B
E/B
feel - ing fine
Well, well, well, he'll make you
Doc-tor
A7
to Φ
Ro-bert
D.S.
Φ Coda
A7
C A7
Ring my friend I said you'd call Doc-tor

A7
Ro-bert
Ring my friend I said you'd call, Doc-tor Ro-bert
Doc-tor Ro-bert
F#7
B
Fade Out

DON'T BOTHER ME

Words & Music by George Harrison.

A7
G7
E7
B7
A7
D
G
to talk to me
me on my own
It's not the same but I'm to blame It's plain to see
It's just not right where ev-ery-night I'm all a - lone
(Straight)
B Em
A
Em
1.
So go a - way (1) and leave me a - lone Don't bo-ther me
I've got no time (2. D.S.) for you right now Don't bo-ther me
I can't be-lieve
2x

2.
Em
C
D
Em
I know I'll ne - ver be the same
If I don't
D.S.x
D.S.x
D.S.x
D.S.x
D
Em
Bm
get her back a - gain
be - cause I know she'll al - ways
D.S.
D.S.
D.S.

Am
C
Em
be
The — on - ly — girl — for — me
But till she's here
D.S.x
D
B7
A7
G7
E7
B7
— please — don't come near — Just stay a - way
I'll let you know — when — she's come home —

A7
D
G
E
Em
A
Till that the day
don't come a-round
Leave me a-lone
don't bo-ther me
D.S.x
to⊕
F
B7
A7
G7
E7
C D
H
S

B7
A7
D
G
I've got no time
Coda
A
Don't bo-ther me
Em
A
Don't bo-ther me
Em
A
Don't bo-ther me
Em
A
Don't bo-ther me
D.S.
Fade Out

DON'T LET ME DOWN

Words & Music by John Lennon & Paul McCartney.

E
A
E
D.S. repeat x
F#m7
F#m7
B
down
Don't let me down
Hey Hey
Don't let me
B
to
1.
(Upper Part D.S.x Tacet)
(1x) No-bo-dy ev-er loved me like she does
(D.S.x) And from the first time that she real-ly done me
Oo she does
Oo she done me
yes she does
she done me good
(Top)

E△7
Esus4
E
F#m7
And if some-bo - dy loved me like she
I guess no-bo - dy ev - er real-ly
do me
done me
Oo she do__ me__
Oo she done__ me__
yes she does_
she done me good_
C
E△7
Esus4
E
2.
E
Don't let me
Don't let me
I'm in love for the first__ time

E
B7
Don't you know it's gon - na last
It's a love that lasts for - ev - er
It's a love that had no past
E
A
E
Don't let me
Coda
D E
(Singing Fake)
Hey
D.S.

F#m7
E
Hey
Ah!
F#m7
E
A
E
Don't let me down

DON'T PASS ME BY

Words & Music by Ringo Starr.

(Straight)
A
C
F
(1X) lis-ten for your foot_ steps
(2X) hear the clock a tick - ing
(D.S.X) sor-ry that I doub- ted you
com-ing up the drive_
on the man-tel shelf_
I was so un-fair_
Lis-ten for your foot_ steps
See the hands a mov - ing
You were in a car- crash
But they don't a-rrive_
But I'm by my-self
And you lost your hair_
I
You
(1x Tacet)
T
A
B
2x
S.D.
D.S.x
G
F
1.
C
Wait-ing for your knock dear
won-der where you are_ to-night
said that you would_ be late
on my old front door_
And why I'm by my-self_
a-bout an hour or two_
I don't
I don't
I said
hear it
see you
that's
Does it mean_ you don't
Does it mean_ you don't
al-right I'm wait-ing_ here just
love me a-ny
love me a-ny
wait-ing to hear from
more_
(1x Tacet)
(2x cruch tacet)

2.
C
C
B
C
I
more
you
Don't pass me by
don't make me cry
don't make me blue
'Cause you know
D.S.x
F
C
G
dar-ling I love on-ly you
you'll ne-ver know it hurt me so
How I hate to see you go
Don't pass me by
T
A
B

G
F
to Φ
C
Don't make me cry
I'm
D.S.x
Φ Coda
D.S.
C
N.C.
G
C
one two three four five six seven eight
wu
Don't pass me by

C
C
F
C
don't make me cry don't make me blue
'Cause you know dar- ling I love on- ly you
You'll ne- ver know it hurt me so
How I
hate to see you go
G
F
Don't pass me by
Don't make me cry
T
A
B

F
C
F
G
Dm7
C
C
Fade Out

DO YOU WANT TO KNOW A SECRET?

Words & Music by John Lennon & Paul McCartney.

(Straight)
B
E G#m Gm F#m B7 E G#m Gm F#m B7 E G#m Gm
Lis-ten do you want to know a sec-ret Do you pro-mise not to tell Wo-w
1x Tacet
do - la - lu do - la - lu do - la -
F#m C E G#m Gm F#m B E G#m Gm F#m B7 A
woh woh clos-er Let me whis-per in your ear Say the words you long to hear
-lu do - la - lu do - la - lu
1x Tacet

B7
C#m
F#m
B7
to Coda C
A
F#m
C#m
Bm
A
F#m
I'm in love with you
oo
I've known a sec-ret for a week or two
No - bo-dy knows
just we two
Coda
oo
D.S.

DRIVE MY CAR

Words & Music by John Lennon & Paul McCartney.

D
G
D
G
She said "ba - by can't you see I wan-na be fa - mous a star of the screen___ But
And she said "ba - by it's un - der - stood Work - ing for pea - nuts is a - ll very fine___ But
And she said "listen baby I've got some-thin' to say I got no car and it's break-ing my heart___ But
A7
B
Bm
G7
Bm
you can do some - thing in be - tween"
I can show you a be - tter time"
I've found a dri - ver and that's a start"
"Ba - by, you can drive my car___ yes, I'm gon-na be a star___
(2,3x)

to 1.
G7
Bm
E7
A7
D
G
A
Ba - by, you can drive my car
And may - be I'll love you"
2.
D
G
A
C
D
G
D
you"
Beep beep mm beep beep, yeah
Q.C
U D
(Tambourine)

G
D
G
A7
Q.C
S
C
U D
(Bottle Neck)
D
Bm
G7
"Baby, you can drive my car
yes, I'm gonna be a star
Baby, you can drive my car

E7
A7
D
G
A
And may-be I'll love ___ you"
Coda
D
G
___ you"
D.S.
Beep beep mm beep beep, yeah ___
Beep beep mm beep beep yeah ___ ,
Beep beep mm beep beep, yeah ___
1X Tacet
1x only
2x only
Fade Out

EIGHT DAYS A WEEK

Words & Music by John Lennon & Paul McCartney.

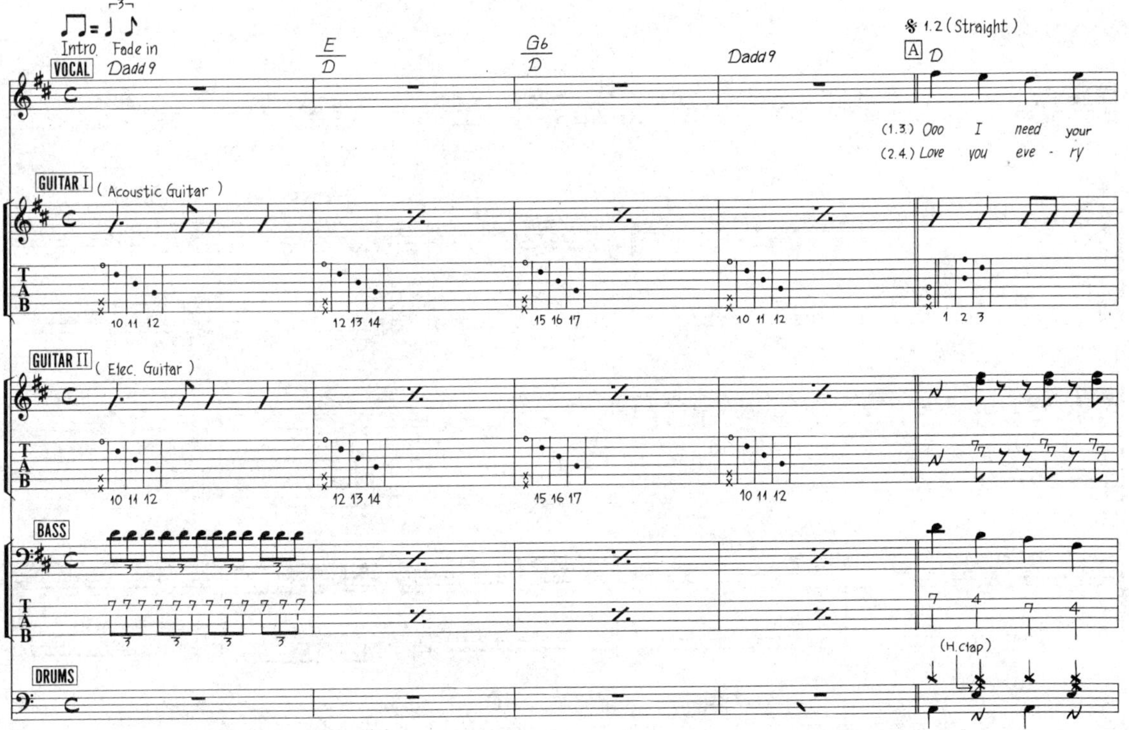

E
G
D
E
love babe___, guess you know it's true___
day girl___, al - ways on my mind___
Hope you need my love babe___,
One thing I can say girl___,
G
D
B Bm
2x, 4x with Chorus
G6
Bm
just like I need you___.
love you all the time___.
Hold me___, love me___, hold me___,
(H.Clap)

E
with chorus
D
E
G
D
D.S. 2 x to
love me, I ain't got no-thing but love, babe, Eight days a week.
C
A
Bm
E
Eight days a week I love you Eight days a

E
G
A
week is not e - nough to show I care
Coda
G
D
Eight day's a week
D.S. 1.2
G
D
D Dadd 9
E/D
G6/D
Dadd 9
eight day's a week

ELEANOR RIGBY

Words & Music by John Lennon & Paul McCartney.

C
Em
Ah, look at all the lone - ly peo - ple
B Em
(1.) E - lea - nor Rig - by Picks up the rice in the church Where a wed - ding has been
(2.) Fa - ther Mc - Ken - zie Writ - ing the words of a ser - mon That no one will hear
(3.) E - lea - nor Rig - by Died in the church and was buri - ed A - long with her name
3x only
2x
3x only
T A B

C Em
Lives in a dream
No-one comes near
No-bo-dy came
Waits at the win - dow
Look at him work - ing
Fa ther Mc-Ken - zie
Wear-ing the face that she keeps
Darn-ing his socks in the night
Wip-ing the dirt from his hands
2x
1x only
2x
3x
(Em7) C
In a jar by the door
When there's no - bo - dy there
As he walks from the grave
C Em
Who is it for
What does he care
No-one was saved
C Em7
All the lone - ly peo -
3x play
Aah, look at all
3x
1x
2x
2x
3x

Em6
C/E
Em
Em7
Em6
- ple Where do they all come from ? All the lone - ly peo - ple Where do
the lone - ly peo - ple
Ah. look at all the lone - ly peo-
2xonly
C/E
to Φ
1.
Em
2.
Em
they all be - long ?
- ple
Φ Coda
Em
D.C.

THE END

Words & Music by John Lennon & Paul McCartney.

B
A
D
A
B
E
A
D
Oh, yeah! All right! Are you gon-na be in my dreams
to-night?
C
A
Q.C

A
D
A7
(E. Guitar)
D7
A7
D7
A7
D7
A7

D7
A7
D7
E
A7
D7
S
H
Q.C
P
T
A
B
(B.G. Simile ~)
(E. Guitar)
A7
D7
A7
D7
C
D
H P
Q.C

A7
D7
A7
D7
A7
D7
A7
D7

A7
D7
A7
D7
8va
F
A
G
A
G
A
And, in the end, The love you take

♩ = ♩.
G/A
F
Dm7
G7
Is e - qual to the love you make.—
(Strings)
H
C
D/C
E♭
F
C
Ah
Brass (8va→)
Strings

EVERYBODY'S GOT SOMETHING TO HIDE EXCEPT ME AND MY MONKEY

Words & Music by John Lennon & Paul McCartney.

B (3times Repeat)
E
A
(1x) come on is such a joy
(2x,3x) come on is such a joy
come on is such a joy
come on is such a joy
come on is take it ea-sy
come on is make it ea-sy
come on is take it ea-sy Take it ea - sy
come on is make it ea-sy Take it ea - sy
3x (Make it)
(1X,3X Bell)
(2X Shaker)
(1X Bell)
(2X,3X Shaker)
D
B7
take it ea - sy
take it ea - sy
Eve-ry - bo-dy's got some-thing to hide ex-cept for me and my

E D G E G D E
1. 2.
C
mo-n-key
Hey
HAH! The deep- er you go the
Your in-side is out and your
8va
(Shaker)
high-er you fly The high-er you fly the deep-er you go So come on Come on
out-side is in Your out-side is in and your in-side is out So come on Ha Come on

D
3.
Hey
E
Come on come on come on come on
come on (Repeat)
Ha
(Bell)
AH
come on (Repeat)
Repeat & Fade Out

EVERYBODY'S TRYING TO BE MY BABY

Words & Music by Carl Lee Perkins.

E
B
A
E
it me
Eve-ry-bo-dy's trying to be my ba-by
Eve-ry-bo-dy's trying to be my ba-by
B7
A
E
C
E
Eve-ry-bo-dy's trying to be my ba-by now
Well, half past nine

D
2.
E
Half past four, fif - ty wom - en knock-ing on my door
A
E

B7
A
E
E
E
Went out last night I
didn't stay late 'fore I got home I had nine - teen dates
A
Eve-ry-bo-dy's trying to be my ba-by

E
B7
A
E
to
Ev-e-ry-bo-dy's trying to be my ba-by Eve-ry-bo-dy's trying to be my___ ba-by now___
F
E
A

E
B7
A
E
G
E
A
8va
8va

E
B7
A
E
Went
D.S.
Coda
E
H
E
Well they took some honey from a tree___ Dressed it up and they called___ it me

A
E
Eve-ry-bo-dy's trying to be my ba-by
Eve-ry-bo-dy's trying to be my ba-by
Eve-ry-bo-dy's trying to
A
E
E7
be my___ ba-by now___

EVERY LITTLE THING

Words & Music by John Lennon & Paul McCartney.

G D A B B7/A E/G# A A
luck - y, Yes, I know I'm a luck- y guy I re - mem- ber the
loves me, Yes, I know that she loves me now There is one thing I'm
Rim.
D E A G D A B B7/A
first time I was lone - ly with - out her, Yes, I'm think - ing a -
sure of I will love her for - ev - er For I know love will

E/G#
A
B A
G
A
- bout her now
nev - er die
Ev'- ry lit - tle thing she does
she does for me, yeah,
A
G
A
To Coda C A
And you know the things she does,
she does for me, woo,

D E
A
G D
A B
B7/A
E/G#
A
D.S.
Coda
A
D E
A
D E
Ev'- ry lit- tle thing
Ev'- ry lit- tle
Repeat & Fade Out

FIXING A HOLE

Words & Music by John Lennon & Paul McCartney.

Fm7
B♭7
Fm7
B♭7
Fm7
stops my mind from wan - der-ing where it will go
B♭7
A
F
Caug
Fm7
Fm6
Fm7
B♭7
I'm fil-ling the cracks that ran through the door and kept my mind from wan - der-ing where it will

B
Fm7
B♭7
Fm7
B♭7
F
C
go
And it real-ly does-n't ma-tter if I'm wrong,
1X Tacet→
uh
F
C
F
C
F
C
G
I'm right where I be-long I'm right where I be-long
See the peo-ple stand-ing there who
Sil-ly peo-ple run a-round they
uh
uh
uh
tu tu tu tu

C
G
C
G
C
C
F
Caug
dis - a - gree and ne - ver win and won - der why they don't get in my door
I'm paint - ing my room in a col -
wor - ry me and ne - ver ask me why they don't get past my door
I'm tak - ing my time for a num -
tu tu tu tu tu tu tu tu uh uh
Fm7
Fm6
Fm7
B♭7
to Φ
Fm7
- our - ful way, and when my mind is wan - der - ing there I will go
- ber of things that weren't im - por - tant yes - ter - day and I still
uh uh uh uh

B♭7
Fm7
B♭7
D
F
Caug
Fm7
Fm6
uh
Hey, hey, hey
hey,
uh
uh
Fm7
B♭7
Fm7
B♭7
Fm7

B♭7
And it
D.S.
Coda
Fm7
go
B♭7
Fm7
uh
uh
uh
uh
B♭7
uh
E
F
Caug
Fm7
Fm6
Fm7
I'm fix-ing a hole where the rain gets in and stops my mind from wand-

B♭7
Fm7
- er - ing where it will___ go
Where it will___ go
I'm
fix-ing a hole___ where the rain___ gets in___ and stops my mind___ from wand - er-ing where it will___ go
Fade Out

FLYING

By John Lennon, Paul McCartney, George Harrison and Richard Starkey.

F7
C
G7
F
C
B
C
(Key Board I)
(Key Board II)

C
F7
C
G7
F
C
G7
C
C
La la la la la

C
C7
F7
La la la la la
La la la la la
C
G7
F
C
La la la la la
Ah
Ah
(Key Board II)
(Key Board I)
H
H

(Free)→
(Key Board)→
8va
tr.
N. C
(Tape Reverse)
8va.
Fade Out

FOOL ON THE HILL

Words & Music by John Lennon & Paul McCartney.

Em7
D
D6
Em7
D
The man with the fool - ish grin is keep - ing per - fect-ly still But
The man of a thou - sand voic - es talk - ing per - fect-ly loud But
2x
4
4
T
A
B
(Straight)
B
Em7
A7
D6
Bm7
no - bo - dy wants to know him they can see that he's just a fool And
no - bo - dy ev - er hears him on the sound he ap - pears to make And
no - bo - dy seems to like him they can tell what he wants to do And
2x
D.S.x
(Harmonica)

Em7
A7
Dm
Dm+5
Dm
Dm+5
he ne - ver gives an ans - wer
he ne - ver seems to no - tice
he ne - ver shows his feel - ings
But the fool on the hill sees the sun go-ing down
(Harmonica)
(Shaker)
(Bell)
C7
Dm
Dm7
And the eyes in his head see the world spin-ning 'round
(2x
2x

D6
D.S.x
C D6
Em7
D
Oh
2x
(Flute II)
(Flute I)
1x Tacet →
D6
Em7
D
to Φ
'round 'round 'round 'round 'round
And
D.S.

Coda
D
Em7
A7
D6
Bm7
Em7
He ne - ver lis - tens to them He knows that they're the fools
But they don't
(Harmonica)
A7
Dm
Dm+5
Dm
Dm+5
C7
like him The fool on the hill sees the sun go-ing down And the eyes in his head
(Harmonica)

C7
Dm
Dm7
D6
E
D6
— see the world___ spin-ning 'round___
oh
(Fl II.)
(Fl. I)
T
A
B
1 2 3
Em7
D
D
Em7
D
'round 'round 'round 'round
oh
Fade Out

FOR NO ONE

Words & Music by John Lennon & Paul McCartney.

B
B
B
F#/A#
G#m
B/F#
lon - ger needs_ you
does - n't need_ him
She wakes_ up, she makes_ up She takes_ her time_ And does-n't feel_
You want_ her, you need_ her And yet_ you don't_ be - lieve her
Your day_ breaks, your mind_ aches There will_ be times_ when all the things_
1x Tacet
3 x only
T
A
B
(1x)
(2x. 3x)
(Tambourine)
E
A
(1x Tacet)
1. 3.
B
C
C#m
G#7
_ she has to hur-ry she no lon-ger needs_ you
When she says her love is dead You
_ She said will fill your head You won't forgot her
And in her eyes_ you see no-thing_

C#m
C#m
G#7
C#m
C#m
F#sus4
F#
No sign of love be-hind the tears
Cried for no-one
A love that should have last-ed years
3x only
1X
3X
Fine
(3X)
2.
B
D
B
F#
A#
G#m
B
F#
E
A
think she needs you

B
E
C#m
G#7
C#m
And in her eyes you see no-thing No sign of love be - hind the tears
T
A
B
C#m
G#7
C#m
C#m
F#
F#sus4
Cried for no - one A love that should have last - ed years
D.C.

FOR YOU BLUE

Words & Music by George Harrison.

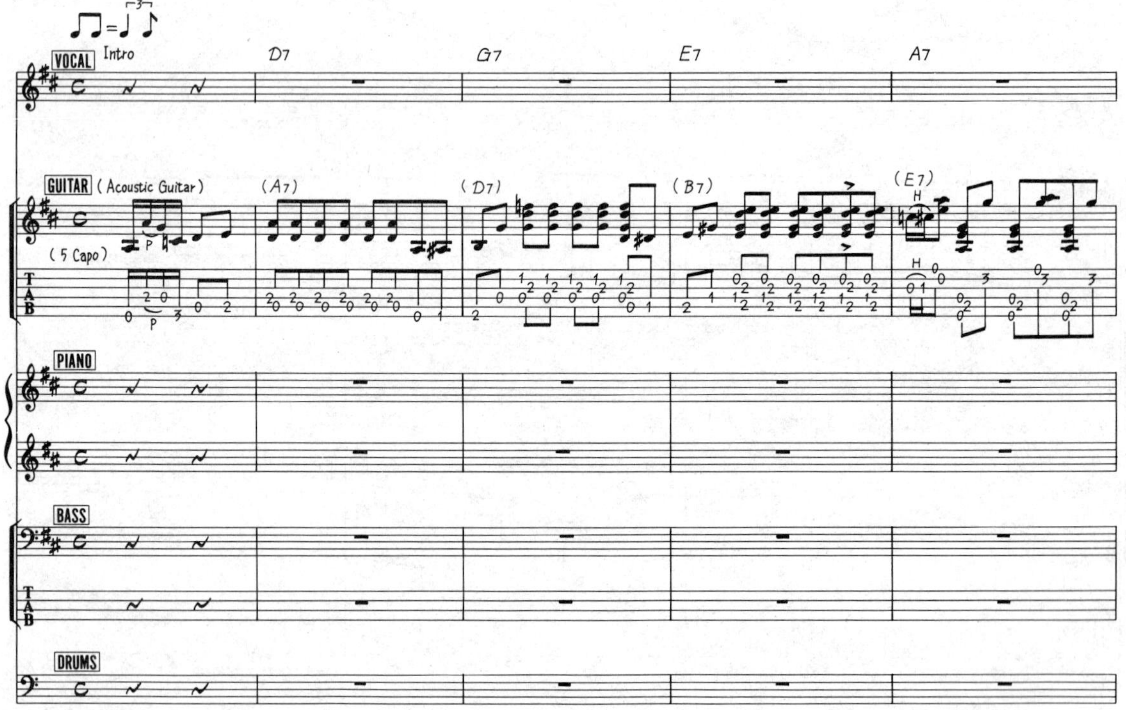

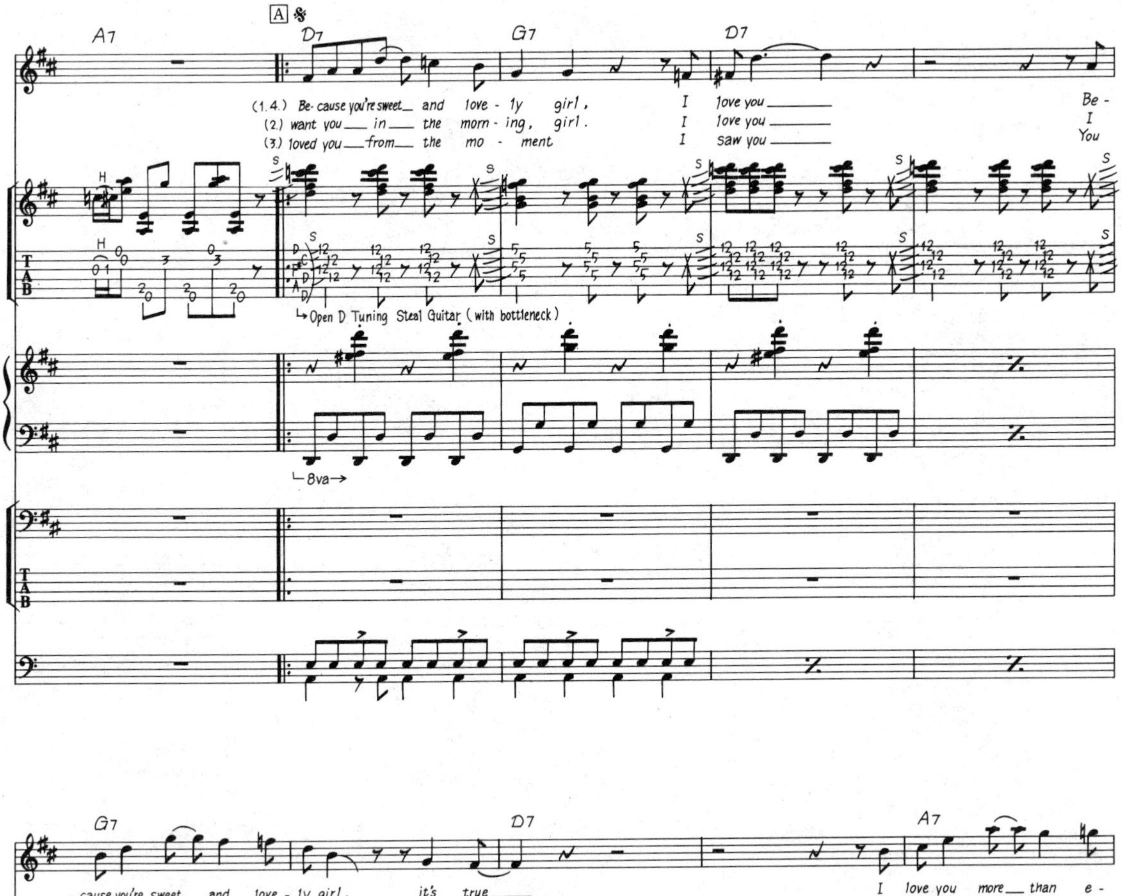

A

A7 D7 G7 D7

(1.4.) Be-cause you're sweet__ and love - ly girl, I love you ____ Be-
(2.) want you __ in __ the morn - ing, girl. I love you ____ I
(3.) loved you __ from __ the mo - ment I saw you ____ You

└ Open D Tuning Steal Guitar (with bottleneck)

└ 8va →

to Φ
1.
2.
G7
D7
A7
D7
A7
-ver, girl, I do
-ment, girl, for you
you feel it too
I
B
D7
G7
D7
G7
Walk
Walk cat walk.

D7
A7
G7
D7
A7
Go John-ny, go.
Same ole tale of blues
C
D7
G7
D7
G7

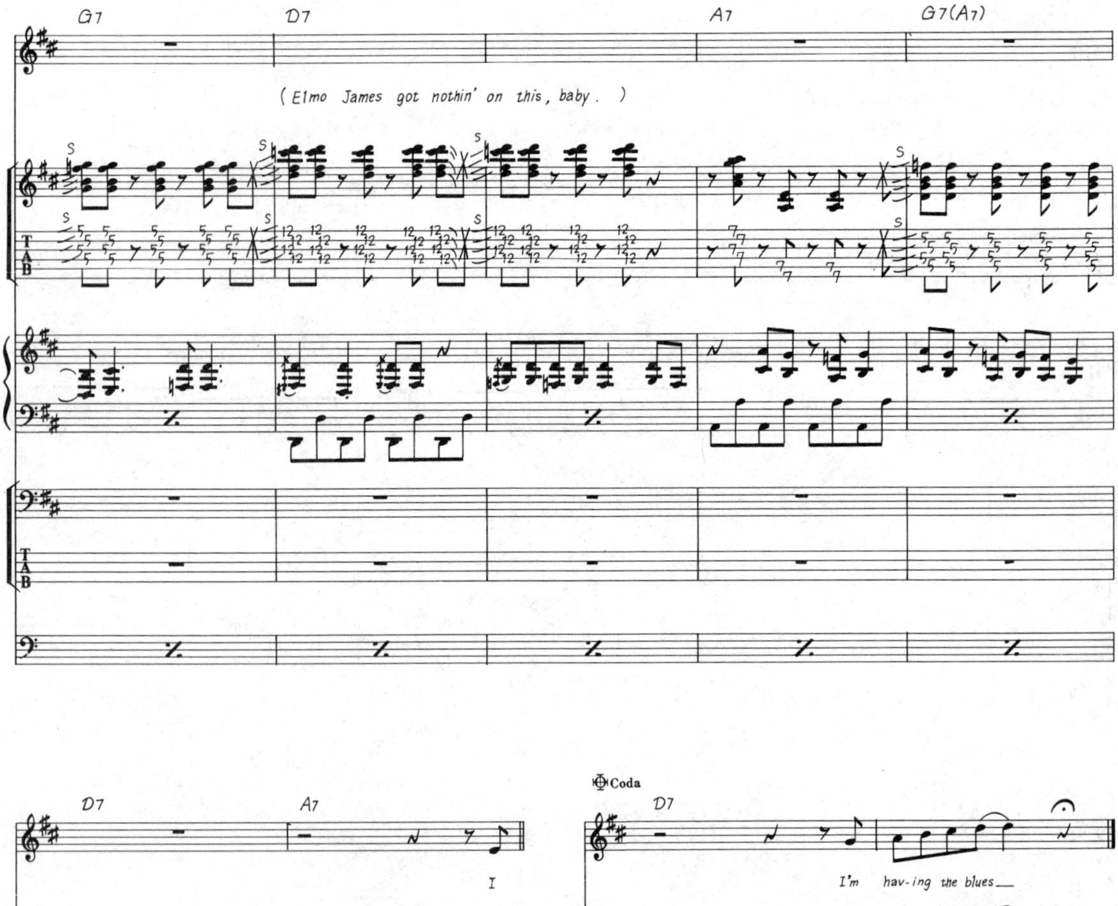

G7 D7 A7 G7(A7)

(Elmo James got nothin' on this, baby.)

FROM ME TO YOU

Words & Music by John Lennon & Paul McCartney.

A
C
Am
G7
F
an-y-thing that you want,
If there's an-y-thing I can do,
Just call on me and I'll
send it a-long with love, from me to you.
to Φ
Vocal 2x tacet
B
I've got ev-'ry-thing that you want,
Like a
2x only
2x only(From me)
2x
S
H
T
A
B

C
G7
2x only
F
Am
C
G7
heart that's oh so true,
2x only (To you)
Just call on me and I'll send it a-long with love, from me to you,
C
Gm7
Upper part. 1x Tacet.
C7
F
I got arms that long to hold you, and keep you by my side I got

D7
G
1.
Gaug
2.
Gaug
lips that long to kiss___ you, and keep you sat - is - fied. Ooo, If there's -fied. Ooo, If there's
Coda
C
Am
A♭aug (E aug)
C
Am
___ To you,___ to you,___ to you.
D.S.

GET BACK

Words & Music by John Lennon & Paul McCartney.

A D A
he was a lon-er But he knew it could-n't last
she was a wom-an But she was an-other man
Jo jo left his home in Tuc-son Ar-i-zo-na for
All the girls a-round her say she's got it com-ing but
C UD
D A B A D
some Cal-i-for-nia-grass
she gets it while she can
Get back! Get back! Get back to where you once be-longed
T A B

A
G/A
D/A
A
D
A
Get back ___ !
Get back ___ !
Get back ___ to where you once be-longed ___
Get back Jo jo !
Get back Loretta !
T A B
1.
A
D
A G D A
C
U D
h.c
Simile～

A
D
A
G
D
C
A
Go home
Get back !
Get back !
Back
D
A
G/A
D/A
A
D
to where you once be-longed
Get back !
Get back !
Back to where you once be-longed

D
D A
Get back Joe
8va
D
A
G/A
D/A
A
H

2.
D
A
G/A
D/A
A
D
A
G/A
D/A
A
D
A
G/A
D/A
Ah, Get back_

E
A
D
A
! Yeah, Get back ! Get back to where you once be-longed Yeah, Get back
A
D
! Get back ! Get back to where you once be-longed Get back Oooh
T
A
B

GETTING BETTER

Words & Music by John Lennon & Paul McCartney.

Dm
G
No I can't com-plain
G
No I can't com-plain
G
Ah
oh
(the) teach-ers who taught me weren't cool
You're hold-ing me down
Burn-ing me round
fill-ing me up with the rules
B
C
Fool - ish rules
Dm
Bet - ter
Em
I've got to ad-mit it's get-ting bet - ter a lit - tle bet - ter all the time
H
T
A
B

F
Can't get no worse
C
Dm
bet-ter
Em
F
I have to admit it's get-ting bet - ter
it's get-ting bet - ter
since you've been mine
4.
G
C
G
Me used to be an - gry young man
me hid-ing me head in the sand
(Piano)

G
You gave me the word I fin-al-ly heard I'm do-ing the best that I can I've
D
C
Dm
C
bet-ter
Em
G
F
Can't get no worse
C
got to admit it's get-ting bet-ter a lit-tle bet-ter all the time I have to admit it's get-ting bet-
(E. Piano)

Dm
C
bet - ter
Em
G
F
- ter It's get-ting bet - ter since you've been mine get - ting so much bet - ter all the time
4.
E
C
Dm
C
Em
G
F
C
It's get-ting bet-ter all the time bet-ter bet-ter bet - ter It's get-ting bet-ter all the

Dm
C
Em
G
F
G
time
bet - ter
bet - ter
bet - ter
I
4.
(Sitar)
T
A
B
Conga
F
G
used to be cruel to my wom - an I beat her and kept her a - part from the things that she loved

G
Fool - ish rules
Man I was mean but I'm chang - ing my scene and I'm do - ing the best that I can
(E. Piano)
G
C
Dm
C
bet - ter
Em
G
F
Can't get no worse
C
I ad - mit It's get - ting bet - ter a lit - tle bet - ter all the time
Yes ad - mit it's get - ting bet -

Dm
C
bet-ter
Em
G
F
- ter it's get-ting bet - ter since you've been mine get - ting so much bet - ter all the time
4.
H
C
Dm
C
Em
G
F
C
It's get-ting bet-ter all the time bet-ter bet-ter bet - ter It's get-ting bet-ter all the

Dm/C
Em/G
F
time___ bet-ter bet-ter___ bet - ter get - ting so much bet - ter all the time__
4.
C
Fade Out

GIRL

Words & Music by John Lennon & Paul McCartney.

E♭ G7 Cm G7 C Cm7 Fm
stay? She's the kind of girl You want so much it makes you sor-ry Still you don't re-gret a sin-gle
cry And she prom-is-es the earth to me and I be-lieve her Af-ter all this time I don't know
said That a man must break his back to earn his day of lei-sure? Will she still be-lieve it when he's
Cm
day
why
dead
B
E♭ Gm Fm B♭7 E♭ Gm
(breathing sound)
to
Ah, Girl oothss Girl Girl
Girl Girl Girl
H.H.

1.
2.
C
Fm
B♭7
C
When I
She's the kind of girl who puts you down When friends are there You feel a
fool
When you say she's look-ing good She acts as if it's un - der-stood she's
tu tu tu tu tu tu tu tu
simile
T.C.

D
Fm
Ab
Eb
Gm
Fm
Bb7
Cool, ooh, ...ooo ...ooo ...ooo
Girl
oothss
Girl
T
A
B
8 9 10
8 9 10 11
6 7 8
10 11 12
8 9 10
8 9 10
H.H.
Eb
Gm
Fm
Bb7
Girl
Girl
Was she
Girl
Girl
Coda
E
Fm
Bb7
Cm
G7
H.H.
T.C.
D.S.

Cm7
Fm
E♭
G7
Cm
G7
Cm7
Fm
Cm
E♭
Gm
Fm
B♭7
Girl
oothss
Girl
Fade Out

GLASS ONION

Words & Music by John Lennon & Paul McCartney.

F7
Am
Gm7
C7(6)
no-thing is re - al
close as can be man
liv-ing there still
Well here's a-no-ther place you can go
Well here's a-no-ther clue for you all
Well here's a-no-ther place you can be
Where
The
D.S.x
(Strings)
2x
2x. D.S.x
(Tambourine)
D.S.x tacet
Gm7
C7
B F7
D7
eve-ry-thing flows
wal-rus is Paul
Lis-ten to me
Look - ing through the bent backed tu - lips
Stand - ing on the cast iron shore yeah
Fix - ing a hole in the oce - an
To
La-
tryin'
A.pf
Contra-Bass.
D.S.x tacet

F7
D7
F7
G
to
1.
see how the o-ther half live
- dy Ma-don-na try-ing to make ends meet yeah
to make a dove-tail joint yeah
Look - ing through a glass oni - on
Look - ing through a glass oni - on
Look - ing through a glass oni - on
1×
D.S.×
2.
G
C Am
F
A
Oh Yeah
On
A.pf.

D7
A
Am7
F7
G
yeah
Oh
Yeah
Look- ing through a glass oni - on
gliss.
D.S.
Coda
D (Slow)
1x only
Repeat & Fade Out

GOLDEN SLUMBERS

Words & Music by John Lennon & Paul McCartney.

G7
C
E7
Am
Dm7
to Φ
Once, there was a way
to get back home.
S-leep pret-ty dar - ling, do not cry,
(2x)
(1x)
H
H
G7
C
B
C
Fadd9
C
And I will sing a lul-la-by
Gold - en slum - bers fill your eyes.

C
Fadd9
C
E7
A7
Dm7
Smiles a-wake you when you rise; S-leep pret-ty dar-ling, do not cry,
H.H.
Cym.
G7
C
And I will sing a lul-la-by.
Coda
G7
C
And I will sing a lul-la-by.
D.S.

GOOD DAY SUNSHINE

Words & Music by John Lennon & Paul McCartney.

F#
B
F#
E
sun - shine,
Good day
sun - shine
Good day
Simile ~
Simile ~
B
1. 3.
A
F#7
B7
E7
sun - shine
(1.) I need to laugh and when the sun is out
(2.) We take a
(3.) Then we lie be-neath a sha - dy tree
I've got some-thing I can
I love her and she's lov-
H.H.

A
A
F#7
B7
E7
to⊕
laugh a - bout I feel good in a spe - cial way I'm in love and it's a
- ing me She feel good She knows she's look-ing fine I'm so prond to know that
T
A
B
5 5 5 5 5 5 2 2 7 7 7 7 0 0 0 0
A
2.
A
F#7
B7
E7
sun-ny day walk the sun is shin - ing down Burns my feet as they touch
T
A
B
5 5 5 5 5 5 2 2 7 7 7 7 0 0 0 0

A
C
D
B7
E7
the ground
A7
D
Coda
A
She is mine
D.S.

D
B
F#
B
F#
Good day___ sun - shine___ Good day___ sun - shine___
T
A
B
7 7 7
2 2 2 2 2
7 7 7
2 2 2 2 2
(with Tambourine)
E
B
F#
Good day___ sun - shine___ Good day___ sun - shine___
0 0 0
0 0 0 0
7 7 7
2 2 2 2 2

B
F#
E
Good day sun - shine
Good day sun - shine
E
F
Good day sun - shine
Good day sun - shine
Good day sun - shine
Good day sun shine
Good day sun -
T
A
B
Fade Out

GOOD MORNING GOOD MORNING

Words & Music by John Lennon & Paul McCartney.

B
A
Em
G
No-thing to do to save his life call his wife in
Af-ter a while you start to smile now you feel cool
No-thing to say but what a day how's your boy
Then you de-cide to take a walk by the old
1x Tacet
been
school
8va
D
E
No-thing to do it's up to you
No-thing has changed it's still the same
I've got
No-thing to say but

1.
C
G
A
D
A
A
Em
G
it's O. K. Good morn-ing good morn-ing good morn-ing a
Go-ing to work don't want to go
8va
T
A
B
feel - ing low down
Head-ing for home you start to roam then you're in town
Em

D
A
D
A
D
A
D
Ev-'ry-bo-dy knows there's no-thing do-ing Ev-'ry-thing is closed it's like a ru-in Ev-'ry-one you see is half a-sleep
A
D
A
2.
A
And you're on your own you're in the street
morn-ing a

E
A
Em
G
A
A
Em
G
A
D
F
A
D
A
D
Peo-ple run-ing 'round___ it's five o'-clock___ Ev-'ry-where in town___ it's get-ting dark___
8va
P+H
P S
H+P
D

A
D
A
D
A
Ev-'ry-one you see
is full of life
It's time for tea
and meet the wife
8va
G
A
Em
G
A
A
Em
G
Some-bo-dy needs
to know
the time
glad
that I'm
here
Watch-ing
the skirts
you start
to flirt

G
A
D
E
now you're in
gear
Go to a show you hope she goes
I've got
8va
A
Em
G
H
A
D
A
no-thing to say but it's O. K. Good
morn-ing good morn-ing good
good
Repeat & Fade Out

GOODNIGHT

Words & Music by John Lennon & Paul McCartney.

Am7
D7
A
G
Bm7
Am7
Am
G
Now it's time to say good night good night sleep tight
(Horn)
T
A
B
G
Bm7
Am7
Am
G
Bm7
Am7
Am
G
D7
Now the sun turns out his light good night sleep tight
(Horn)
7
10

GΔ7
D7/G
GΔ7
D7/G
G
C/G
G
C/G
B
G
Bm7
Dream sweet dreams for me,
Dream sweet dreams for you.
Close your eyes and
Close your eyes and
(Harp)
(Horn)
Am7
Am/G
Bm7
Am7
Am/G
D7
G
Bm7
Am7
Am/G
I'll close mine good night sleep tight Now the moon be-gins to shine
I'll close mine good night sleep tight Now the sun turns out his light
(Flute)
(Horn)

Bm7
Am7
C/G
D7
GΔ7
D7/G
to ⊕
GΔ7
D7/G
G
C/G
good night sleep tight Dream sweet dreams for me.
Dream sweet dreams for
good night sleep tight Dream sweet dreams for
(Harp)
T A B
9 9 7 7
10 10 9 10
10 10 10 10 10 7
10 10 9 10 10 7
10 10 10 10 10 7
G
C/G
C
G
Am7
A7
Dm7
G7
C/G
D
Am
D7
you
mm
mm
mm
10 10 10 10 8
D.S.

Coda
GΔ7
D7/G
G
C/G
G
C/G
D
G
Bm7
me.
Dream sweet dreams for you
(Flute)
(Harp)
Am7
D7
G
Bm7
Am7
D7
G
(Whispered) Good night good night ev-'ry-bo-dy ev-'ry-bo-dy ev-'ry-where good night.
(Flute)
(Horn)

GOT TO GET YOU INTO MY LIFE

Words & Music by John Lennon & Paul McCartney.

G
F/G
G
I did-n't know what I would find there
You knew I wanted just to hold you
When I'm with you I want to stay there
A - no-ther road where may-be I
And had you gone, you knew in time
If I'm true I'll ne-ver leave
Simile
F/G
Bm
Bm△7/B♭
could see a-noth-er kind of mind there
We'd meet a-gain for I had told you
And if I do I know the way there
(1.3.) Ooo
(2.) Ooo
then I sud-
you were meant

Bm7/A
Bm6/Ab
Bm
BmΔ7/Bb
Bm7/A
Bm6/Ab
C
Em7/B
- den - ly see you Ooo
did I tell you I need you
Eve - ry sin - gle
to be near me Ooo
and I want you to hear me
Say we'll be to -
Am7
D7
G
1.
2.
G
B
G
day of my life?
ge - ther eve - ry day
Got to get you in - to my life

C
to Φ
D
G
T
A
B
D.S.
Φ Coda
D
G
I
H
C

C
G
C
D
G
got to get you in-to my life
D
G
I was a-lone, I took a ride I did-n't know what I would find there A-

G
- no-ther road where may-be I could see a-no-ther kind of mind there
Ooo then I sud-den-ly see you

did I tell you I need you
Eve-ry sin-gle day
Fade Out

HAPPINESS IS A WARM GUN

Words & Music by John Lennon & Paul McCartney.

B
Dm6
Am
She's well ac-quain-ted with the touch of the vel - vet hand Like a liz-ard on a win - dow pane The
Dm6
Am
Dm6
man in the crowd with the mul-ti-co-lored mir-ror on his hob - nail boots
Ly - ing with his eyes while his hands are bu - sy work-ing

Am
o - ver time
Dm6
A soap im-pres-sion of his with which he ate and do-na-ted to the
Am
Natio-nal Trust
C
A7
C
Am
1hc

D
A7
C
Am
I need a Fix 'cause I'm going down
Down to the bits that I left up - town
I need a Fix 'cause I'm going down
E (3 times)
A7
C
1 x upper part tacet
Mo-ther Su-per-ior jump the gun
A7
G7
Mo-ther su-per-ior jump the gun
F
C
Am
Hap-pi-ness is a
Hap-pi-ness
do
H.H
2x, 3x
2x, 3x Tambourine

F G C Am F G G C Am F G
warm gun Hap-pi-ness is a warm gun Ma-ma When I hold you in my arms
Bang Bang shoot Hap-pi-ness Bang Bang shoot shoot oh
do do do do do do do do do
C Am F G C Am F G H C Am F G C Am
And I feel my fin-ger on your trig-ger I know no-bo-dy can do no harm Be-cause is a warm gun Ma-ma Hap-pi-ness is a
Yeah wu oh Yeah wu oh Yeah Hap-pi-ness Bang Bang shoot shoot Hap-pi-ness
do do do do do do do do do do do

(a tempo)
F
G
Fm
C
(Free)
I
C
Am
warm gun Yes it is
Hap-pi-ness is a warm
Yes it is gun
Bang Bang shoot shoot
Hap-pi-ness
do do
do
F
G
C
Am
F
G
C
Ah, don't you know that hap-pi-ness
is a warm gun Ma-ma
Bang Bang shoot shoot Hap-pi-ness
is a warm gun Yeah
do do do do do

A HARD DAY'S NIGHT

Words & Music by John Lennon & Paul McCartney.

G
C
G
F
G
Hard Day's Night
I should be sleep-ing like a log
But when I
worth it just it hear you say
you're gon-na give me ev'-ry-thing
So why I
(Straight)
B
C
D
G
C7
1.
G
(1x) get home to you I find the things that you do will make me feel al - right
You know I
(2x, D.S.x) love to come home 'cause when I get you a-lone You know I feel o - kay
D.S.x
2x, D.S.x

2.
G
C Bm
Em
Bm
D.S.x
when I'm home
ev'-ry-things seems to be al-right (D.S.x)
when I'm home
G
Em
C7
D7
feel-ing you hold-ing me tight
tight
Yeah It's been a
D.S.x
B. Dr.

D
G C G F G G C
Hard Day's Night___ and I've been work-ing_____ like a dog_____ It's been A Hard Day's Night_
G F G C
___ I should be slee-ping_______ like a log_______ But when I get home to you I find the
D.S.(__ a log___)

D
G
C7
to Φ
G
E
G
C
G
things that you do will make me feel al - right Oh!
F
G
G
C
G

F
G
So why I
D.S.
Coda
G
G
C
You know I feel al - right
G
C
G
C
Fadd9
D
F
D
You know I feel al - right
(Arpeggio)
(Arpeggio)
Repeat & Fade Out

HELLO GOODBYE

Words & Music by John Lennon & Paul McCartney.

G7
Am
G7
G7
C/G
G7
Oh no
You say good-bye and
U D
10 10
P
2X
(Top)
F/G
1. 2.
B
C
C/B
Am7
Am7/G
F
A♭6
I say hel-lo
hel-lo hel-lo
I don't know why you say good-bye I say hel-lo
2X only (Chorus) Hel-lo Good-bye Hel-lo Good-bye
Hel-lo Good-bye
(Top)

C
C/B
Am7
Am7/G
F
B♭9
to ⊕ 1. 2.
1.
C
hel-lo hel-lo
I don't know why you say good-bye I say hel-lo
Organ Hel-lo Good-bye Hel-lo Good-bye
Hel-lo Good-bye
Hel-lo Good-bye
2.
C
C
F6
C
G7
why why why why why why do you say
(Organ)

Am
G7
echo
D
Am
G7
good-bye
good-bye
bye bye bye bye
Oh
no
G7
C
G
G7
F
G
You
say good-bye
and
I
say hel-lo
Coda 1.
C
E
F6
You say
yes
(Chorus)
I
say yes
(Organ)
D.S. 1.

C
G7
Am
G7
I say no
You say stop
And I say go go go
Ah
But I may mean no
I can stay till it's time to go
(Fidle)
Am
G7
G
C
G
G7
F
G
Oh no
You say good-bye and I say hel-lo
D.S. 2.

Repeat & Fade Out

HELP!

Words & Music by John Lennon & Paul McCartney.

E7
A7
B
A
need some - one
(1x) When I was young - er so much
(2x) And now my life has changed in
Help
(1x) When when I was
(2x) Now my life has
(Body Slap)
(H.H.)
C#m
F#m
D
G
young - er than to - day
oh so ma - ny ways
I ne - ver need - ed an - y - bo - dy's help in an - y - way
My in - de - pen - dence seems to va - nish in the haze
young I ne - ver need help in an - y - way
changed my in - de - pend va - nish in the haze
2x

A
C
A
C#m
(1X, D.S.X) But now these days are gone I'm not so self - as -
(2X) But ev' - ry now and then I feel so in - se -
(1X, D.S.X) Now these days are gone
(2X) But now and then
D.S. time no H.H.
D.S.X
(Tambourine)
F#m
D
G
- sured Now I find I've changed my mind I've op - end up the doors
- cure I know that I just need you like I've ne - ver done be - fore
And now I find I've op - ened up the doors
I know I that I've ne - ver done be - fore
no H.H.

A
D
Bm
Help me if you can I'm feel - ing down
And I do
Guitar III
(Top)
D.S.x
G
E7
ap - pre - ci - ate you be - ing round
Help me get my feet
Help me get my feet

E7
A7
to Φ
back on the ground
Won't you please please help
me
back on the ground
Won't you please please help
me
Body Slap
A
E
A
C#m
When I was young - er so much young - er than to - day
(TOP)
(TOP center)

C#m
F#m
D
G
A
I ne-ver need-ed any-y-bo-dy's help in an-y-way
D.S.
Coda
F#m
A
A♭
me
me!
me!
Oo
me
Help
Help
me
Oo
(TOP)

HELTER SKELTER

Words & Music by John Lennon & Paul McCartney.

E+5
G
to 1. E7
Till I get to the bot-tom and I see you a-gain
Yeah Yeah Yeah
D.S.1x
(chorus)
Yeah
(H.H. Open)
B
E7
Do you don't you want me to love you
I'm com-ing down fast but I'm mi-les a-bove you
AH

E7
G
A
Tell me tell me tell me come on tell me the an-swer
and you may be a lo-ver but you ain't no dan -
AH
E7
C
A
E7
A
- cer
Go Hel - ter Skel - ter
Hel - ter Skel - ter
Hel - ter Skel - ter
da da da da da da da

E7
to Coda 2
E7
𝄋 2. (with repeat)
D E7
Yeah
Hu
Hu
I will you won't you want me to make you
2x (Ooh)
D.S.2X (do you don't)
I'm com-ing down fast but don't let me break you
D.S.2X (you)
G
Tell me tell me tell me the an-swer you
AH
AH
D.S. 2x only
8va
gliss.
D.S. 2x

A
E7
2.
E7
may be a lov-er but you ain't no dan - cer
D.S.2x (ain't no dan - cer)
Look out
Look out cause here she comes
da da da da da da da
Feed Back
E
A
E7
A
E7
When I
AH
AH
Feed Back
8va
Coda 1.
E7
Well
Yeah
D.S. 1.
D.S. 2.

Coda 2 F
E7
Hel-ter_Skel-ter
She's com-ing down fast
Yes
she is
Yes_ she is
com-ing down fast
Guitar II
8va
Guitar III
wu
(Slow)
8va
Slide
Slide
roll.
Dubbing Tom

a Tempo
G E7
(2x Fade In)
Brass Fake
Feed Back
Feed Back
1.

2.
E7
Brass Fake
Brass Fake
Fade Out
(Slow)
(Shout)
Roll

HERE COMES THE SUN

Words & Music by George Harrison.

A
D
E7
A
A
Here comes the sun do do do do
D
G
D
D
B7
A
D
A
C#
Bm7
A
E
Here comes the sun, and I say It's all right
G
E7
D
G
D
F#
Em7
D
A

B
A
D
E7
A
Lit - tle dar - ling It's been a long cold lone - ly win - ter Lit - tle dar - ling
Lit - tle dar - ling The smiles re - turn - ing to the fac - es Lit - tle dar - ling
Lit - tle dar - ling I feel that ice is slow - ly melt - ing Lit - tle dar - ling
(D.S.X)
(2X)
D
G
A7
D
T
A
B
It feels like years since it's been here
It seems like years since it's been here
It seems like years since it's been clear
Here come the sun do do do do
D.S.X only
(2X, 3X)
G
A7
D

D
B7
A
D
A/C#
Bm7
A
E
to
Here come the sun, and I say "It's all right"
(D.S.x)
(1x, 2x)
G
E7
D
G
D/F#
Em7
D
A
1.
2.
A
E7
E7
E7
C
G
D
A7
A7
A7
F
C

D
A
E7
E7
C
Sun,
(5x)8va
(4x,5x)
(3x,4x)
G
D
A7
A7
F
Synth. 1x Tacet
G
D
1.2.3.4.
A
E7
E7
sun,
sun,
here it
comes
(3x)
(2x,4x)
(Synth)
C
G
D
A7
A7

5.
A
E7
Esus4
E7
comes
D
A7
Asus4
A7
D.S.
Coda
A
D
B7
Here comes the sun do do do do
Here comes the sun
D
G
E7

A
D
A/C#
Bm7
A
E
A
"It's all ___ right"
It's all ___ right
D
G
D/F#
Em7
D
A
D
D
A/C#
Bm7
A
E
C
G
D
rit. - - -
A
G
D/F#
Em7
D
A
F
C
G
D

HERE, THERE AND EVERYWHERE

Words & Music by John Lennon & Paul McCartney.

Bm
C
G
Am
Bm
C
F#m
B7
mak - ing each day of the year
run - ning my hands through her hair
Chang - ing my life with a wave of her hand
Both of us think - ing how good it can be
Woo
Woo
Woo
Woo
Woo
Woo
Woo
F#m
B7
Em
Am
1.
Am7
D7
2.
Am7
D7
F7
No - bo - dy can de - ny That there's some - thing there
Some - one is speak - ing but she does - n't know he's there
I want her

C
B♭ Gm Cm D7 Gm Cm D7
every-where And if she's be-side me I know I need ne-ver care But to love her is to need her
G Am Bm C G Am Bm C F#m B7
eve-ry - where Know-ing that love is to share Each one be-liev - ing that love ne-ver dies
2x
Woo Woo Woo Woo Woo Woo Woo Woo Woo

F#m
B7
Em
Am
to ⊕
Am7
D7
F7
2x
Watch-ing her eyes
And hop-ing I'm al - ways there
I want her
Woo
Woo
Woo
⊕ Coda
Am7
D7
I will be
Woo
D.S.
D
G
Am
Bm
C
G
Am
Bm
C
G
there
and ev-e - ry-where
Here, there and ev-e - ry-where
Woo
Woo
Woo
Woo
Woo
Woo
Woo
Woo
Woo

HER MAJESTY

Words & Music by John Lennon & Paul McCartney.

A7
Bm
I wan - na tell her that I love her a lot but I
D7
G
Em
G
D
B7
got - ta get a bel - ly full of wine.
Her Ma - jes - ty's a pret - ty nice girl, some - day
Em7
A7
D
B7
Em7
A7
D
I'm gon - na make her mine Oh yeah, Some - day I'm gon - na make her mine.

HEY BULLDOG

Words & Music by John Lennon & Paul McCartney.

N.C.
(Straight)
A
B
F#m7
Sheep dog
Child-like
Big man
standing in the rain
no one un-der-stands
walk-ing in the park
B
F#m7
A
F#m7
Bull-frog
Jack-knife
Wig-wam
do-ing it a-gain
in your swea-ty hands
fright-ened of the dark
Some kind of hap-pi-ness is
Some kind of in-no-cence is
Some kind of so-li-tude is

E
E7
A
F#m7
B
- meas - ured out in miles
- meas - ured out in years
- meas - ured out in you
What makes you think you're some - thing spe - cial when you smile
You don't know what it's like to lis - ten to your fears
You think you know it but you have-'nt got a clue
1x Tacet
1x Tacet
B
Bm
Bm+5
Bm6
Bm7
Em
Em+5
Em6
Em7
You can talk to me
you can talk to me
You can talk to me if you're
Dubbing Snare

Bm
Em
C
N.C.
yeah
lone-ly you can talk to me
D.S. time 8va. bassa.
D.S.x
D.S.x
to⊕
D
B
F#7
(Speaking ~)
H
H
D.S.x

B
F#m7
A
F#m7
E
E7
S
S
H
H
H
D.S.
Coda
E
B
F#m7
(Upper Part 1X Tacet)
1 x Tacet
- dog
Hey Bull -
gliss
gliss
Repeat & Fade Out

HEY JUDE

Words & Music by John Lennon & Paul McCartney.

B♭
F
C7
to
1.
F
- mem - ber to let her in - to your heart then you can start to make it bet - ter Hey
min - ute you let her un - der your skin then you be - gin to make it bet -
- mem - ber to let her in - to your heart then you can start to make it bet -
- mem - ber to let her un - der your skin then you be - gin to make it bet -
D.S.2X
(2x) Ah
bet -
- mem - ber you let her in - to your heart then you can start to make it bet -
- mem - ber to let her un - der your skin then you be - gin to make it bet -
D.S.2X
T
A
B
1 2 3
2.
F
F7
B
B♭
B♭/A
Gm
Gm7/F
- ter And a - ny - time you feel the pain Hey Jude re - frain don't car - ry the world
- ter So let it out and let it in Hey Jude be - gin you're wait - ing for some -
- ter
- ter
Ah
1 2 3 4
3 4 5
(1x Tacet)
(Top)
D.S.1X

C7/E
C7
F
F7
B♭
B♭/A
up - on your shoul - ders
- one to per - form with
For now you know that it's a fool who plays it cool
And don't you know that it's just you Hey Jude you'll do
Oh
D.S.1x Electric Guitar
D.S.1x
Gm
Gm7/F
C7/E
C7
F
F7
By mark - ing his world a lit - tle cold - er
The move - ment you need is on your shoul - der
Da da da da da
Da da da da da
1x, D.S.1x Electric Guitar

C7
da da da da
da da da da yeah
Hey
Hey Jude
D.S. 1.
2.
Coda
F
ter bet-ter bet-ter bet-ter bet-ter bet-ter oh
ter bet-ter bet-ter bet-ter bet-ter be-ter oh
(Tambourine)
C
F
1x Yeah
3times
yeah, yeah yeah yeah yeah yeah
E♭
B♭
F
(Chorus) Da da da dadada da Da da da da Hey Jude
1x
(Contra Bass)
3X
2X, 3X
(Top)
(Tambourine)
(Hand Clap)

D
4 times
2x(Ah - u Ah - u
Da da da
E♭
dadada da
Ah-u Ho Da da da
B♭
Dadada da
F
1x(Ju Ju - de Ju - de Ju-de Ju-de Ju-de)
Hey Jude
(Strings Section)
(Contra Bass)
E
(Ah oh Jude)
Da da da dadada da
Da da da da
2X
Hey Jude
2x(Jude Jude Jude Jude Jude Jude)
(Horn Section I)
(Strings)
(Horn Section II)
(Contra Bass)
(Strings Section)
Repeat & Fade Out

HOLD ME TIGHT

Words & Music by John Lennon & Paul McCartney.

F
B♭7
G7
D.S.1. D.S.2x
C7
chorus
Hold
F7
me tight
then, I might
-night to-night
Ne-ver be the lone-ly one, So
Mak-ing love to on-ly you, So
Hold me tight to-night
2x D.S.1x
B♭
to-night
B♭m
to-night
It's you
You you you oo-oo-oo-oo
to
1.
C7
2x
D.S.1x
D.S.2x
D.S.2

2.
A♭
B F
A♭7
F
B♭7
D.S.1x
Gm
- oo Don't know what it means to hold you tight Be-ing here a-lone to-night with you
G7
C7
D.S.1x
Coda
A♭
F
A♭
rit.
F
If feels al-right now
oo - oo - oo You oo - oo
D.S. 1.
2. (al Coda)

HONEY DON'T

Words & Music by Carl Lee Perkins.

(Straight)
A
E
C
come you say you will when you won't? Say you do, ba-by when you don't.
love you, ba-by, and you ought to know. I like the way that you wear your clothes.
some-times I love you on a Satur-day night. Sun-day morning you don't look right.
T
A
B
1 2 3
E
C
B7
Let me know, ho-ney, how you feel. Tell the truth now, is love real? so aw, aw,
E-very-thing a-bout you is so dog-gone sweet. You got that sand all o-ver your feet, so Aw, aw,
You been out paint-ing the town. Uh-huh, baby you been slipp-ing a-round. so Aw, aw,

B7
E
B E
Well___, ho-ney, don't___.
Well___, ho-ney, don't___.
Well___, ho-ney, don't___.
Well___, ho-ney, don't___
ho-ney, don't___
I say__, ho-ney don't___
Ho-ney don't_
A7
E
Ho-ney don't___
Ho-ney don't___

B7
E
to
I say you will when you won't
Aw , aw , ho- ney don't
Well, I
C
E
C
E

C
B7
D
E
I feel fine
A7
E
B7
A
B
Ooo
oo
I say

E
Well___,
D.S.
Coda E
E
C
E
C
B7
F E

E
A7
Well, ho-ney don't.
Well, ho - ney, don't
a lit - tle, lit - tle, ho - ney
E
B7
E
don't
I say, you will when you won't,
Aw, aw, ho - ney, don't

HONEY PIE

Words & Music by John Lennon & Paul McCartney.

Am
D
Cm
G
A7
time
In the U. S. A.
And if she could on - ly hear me
Harm.
tr.
H
D7
this is what I'd say ;
B Medium Bounce
G
Hon - ey Pie
Hon - ey Pie
You are mak - ing me
My po - si - tion is
1 x Tacet
S
(Brush)

1.
2.
C
Eb7
E7
A7
D7
G
F#
F
Em
cra - zy
I'm in love, but I'm
la - zy
So won't you please come
home .
tra - gic
Come and show, me the
ma - gic
(1 X Tacet)
on
of your Hol - ly-wood song
You be-came a leg -
Will the wind that blew
T
A
B

C#m7-5
G
G7
C
E7/B
- end of the sil - ver screen,
And now the thought of meet - ing you makes me weak in the knee.
her boat a-cross the sea,
kind - ly send her sail - ing back to me.
8 9 10
7 8 9
Am
D7
D
G
Eb7
oh Hon-ey Pie
You are driv - ing me fran - tic.
T. T. Tee, Now Hon-ey Pie
You are mak - ing me cra - zy.
5 6 7
5 6 7
3 4 5
4 5 6

E7
A7
D7
To Coda
G
E♭7
D7
Sail a-cross the At-lan - - tic,
To be where you be - long
Hon-ey Pie, come back to me,
I'm in love but I'm la - - zy,
So, won't you please come home
E
G
E♭7
E7
A7
D7

G
E♭7
D7
F
G
E♭7
E7
A7
D7
G
F#
F
D.S.

Coda
G
E♭7
D7
G
E♭7
Come, come back to me, Hon-ey Pie. Ha ha ha
T
A
B
3 4 5
4 5 6
3 4 5
3 4 5
4 5 6
E7
A7
D7
G
E♭7
D7
G
Hon - ey Pie, Hon-ey Pie
5 6 7
5 6 7
3 4 5
3 4 5
4 5 6
3 4 5
3 4 5

I AM THE WALRUS

Words & Music by John Lennon & Paul McCartney.

𝄋 2.
A
D
D7
A
A/G
C
D
D/E
(1x) I am he as you are he as you are me and we are all to-ge-
(2x) Mis-ter ci-ty p'lice-man sit-ting pret-ty lit-tle p'lice-man in a row
(D.S.2x) Ex-pert tex-pert chok-ing smok-ers don't you think the jo-ker laughs at you
A
A/G
C
D
-ther
See how they run like pigs from a gun see how they fly I'm
See how they fly like Lu-cy in the sky see how they run I'm
See how they smile like pigs in a sty; see how they hide I'm
D.S.2x Chorus
1x Horn
2x

B
A
A/G
D9/F#
F
G
cry - - ing
(1X) Sit-ting on a corn-flake
wait-ing for the van to come
I'm (D.S.1X) Yel-low mat-ter cus-tard
drip-ping from a dead dog's eye
(D.S.2X) sem-o-li-na pil-chards
climb-ing up the Eif-fel Tow-er
D.S. 1x Horn.
D.S. 2x
2x
Cor-po-ra-tion tee shirt stu-pid bloo-dy Tues-day man you been a naugh-ty boy you let your face grow long
Crab-a-lock-er fish-wife por-no-graph-ic pries-tess boy you been a naugh-ty girl you let your Knick ers down
El-e-men-t'ry pen-guin sing-ing Ha-re Krish-na man you should have seen them Kick-ing Ed-gar Al-lan Poe
I am the

to 1. 2.
C
2.
C
D
E
D.S. 2x
Dsus4
egg - man
they are the egg - man
I am the wal - rus
Goo goo g' joob
cry
D.S 2X(joob goo goo)
Chorus
D.S. 2x
(Chorus)
D.S. 1x, D.S. 2x
D.S. 2x
T
A
B
A
E
D
- ing I'm cry - - ing
I'm cry
ing
(Melotoron)
D.S. 1

Coda 1.
E
D B
A
G
F
E
E B
A
Sit-ting in an Eng - lish gar-
(Bell)
G
F
E
F
B
- den wait-ing for the sun
If the sun don't come you get a tan from stand-ing in the Eng-lish rain
I am the

C
D
E
D
egg - man
they are the egg - man
I am the wal - rus
Goo goo g' joob g' goo — goo g' joob —
D.S. 2.
Coda 2.
D
C
B
— goo g' joob —
Goo goo g' goo g' goo — goo g' joob goo —
ju-ba ju-ba ju-ba

F
A
2x Tacet
G
F
E
ju-ba ju-ba ju-ba ju-ba ju-ba ju-ba ju-ba
ju-ba ju-ba
(Speaking)
(Rhythmical speaking)
2x
D
C
B
Repeat & Fade Out

I CALL YOUR NAME

Words & Music by John Lennon & Paul McCartney.

A
E7
C#7
F#7
but you're not there,
Was I to blame,
for be-ing un-fair,
B7
E7
C#7
Oh I can't sleep at night
Since you've been gone,
I ne-ver

F♯7
A
Am
E7
B
A7
weep at night
I can't go on.
Well don't you know I can't take it,
C♯m
F♯7
C7
I don't know who can,
I'm not goin' to Ma - - - -ke it
I'm not that kind of man.

B7
C
E7
C#7
F#7
A
Oh I can't sleep at night, But just the same I nev-er weep at night
Am
to
E7
D
E7
I call your name. (Wow)
C
U D P
S
1 2 3
2 3 4
2 3 4 5

C#7
F#7
A
Am
E7
Coda
E7
A7
E
E7
A7
Well don't you know I can't
I call your name
I call your name
D.S.
Repeat & Fade Out

I DON'T WANT TO SPOIL THE PARTY

Words & Music by John Lennon & Paul McCartney.

D/E
D/F#
G
𝄋 1. 3.
A G
I don't (1.3.) want to spoil the par - ty so I'll go
(2.4.) had a drink or two and I don't care
I would hate my dis - ap - point - ment to show
There's no fun in what I do if she's not there
D

D
B
Em
woo
B7
woo
Am7
woo
D
There's nothing for me here, So I will dis-ap-pear. if she turns
I won-der what went wrong, I've wait-ed far too long. I
4x(if I think
1 2 3
G
Fadd 9
G
to
1.
3.
1.
2.
G
up while I'm gone, please let me know.
think I'll take a walk and look for her.
)
I've
Though to-night
1 2 3

(with Repeat & to D.S. 3.)
C
G
Em
A
C
she's made me sad,
I
still
love
her I'll be glad,
I
still
love
1.
2.
D
D
her
If I
find
her
I
don't
Coda 1.
G
D
G
D.S. 1. al Coda 1.
D.S. 3. al Coda 3.

G
D
Em
B7
Am
D
G
Fadd9

G
Though to-night
D.S. 2.
Coda 3.
G
E
G
Fadd9
D
D
G

I FEEL FINE

Words & Music by John Lennon & Paul McCartney.

G
A
(Straight)
G7
(1.) Ba - by's good to me you know, She's hap - py as can be, You know, She said so
(2.3.) Ba - by says she's mine, you know, She tells me all the time, You know, She said so
D7
C7
I'm in love with her and I Feel
I'm in love with her and I Feel
T.C
Rim Shot

1.
G7
2.
G7
B
G
Bm
Fine.
Fine.
I'm so glad that
Fine.
Fine.
I'm so glad
C
D7
G
Bm
Am
D7
She's my lit-tle girl
She's so glad she's tell-ing all the world
That her ba-
Ooo
She's so glad
Ooo

C
G7
D7
- by buys her things___ you know___ He buys her dia - mond rings___ you know,__ She said___ so.
C7
G7
D
G7
She's in love with me___ and I__ Feel__ Fine mm______
She's in love with me___ and I__ Feel__ Fine
H
S

G7
D7
E
D7
C7
G7
D.S.

Repeat & Fade Out

IF I FELL

Words & Music by John Lennon & Paul McCartney.

E♭m
D
Em7
A7
been in love be-fore And I found that love was more that just hold-ing hands
If I
B
1.(Straight)
2.
D
Em
F♯m
Fdim
Em7
A7
D.S.1x
(1x) give my heart to you I must be sure from the
(2x) trust in you oh please don't run and hide if I
(D.S.1x, D.S.2x) hope you see that I would love to love you
(Arpeggio)
(Rim)

D
Em
F#m
Fdim
Em7
to ⊕
A7
D.S.1X
1.
D
ve - ry start that you would love me more that her
love you too oh please don't hurt my pride like
and that she will cry when she learns we are two
Gm
A7
C
2.
D9
G
If I her
'cause I could - n't stand the pain
And I

Gm
D
A7
would be sad If our new love was in vain So I
D.S. 1. 2. al Coda
Coda
A7
D
Gm
D
Gm
D
she learns we are two If I fell in love with you
Guitar II Harmonics
Guitar III Harmonics

IF I NEEDED SOMEONE

Words & Music by George Harrison.

A
G
A
- one to love You're the one That I'd be think - ing of
If I need - ed some-
A
- one
(Straight)
B
A
(1.3.) If I had some more time to spend
(2.) Carve your num - ber on my wall And
(H.H.)

A
G/A
Then I guess I'd be with you my friend
may-be you will get a call from me
If I need-ed some-one
1.3.
C Em
F#7
Bm
Had you come some o-ther day Then it might not have been like this
(Tambourine)

Em
F#7
Bm
to⊕
Esus4
E7
But you see now I'm too much in love
2.
A
D
A
Ah
Ah
(Arpeggio)
Simile
(T.C.)

G
A
A
Ah
Ah
D.S.
Coda
Esus4
E7
E
A
(4.) Carve your num - ber on my wall And may - be you will get

A
G/A
A
— a call — from me —
If I need - ed some - one
F
Ah
Ah

I'LL BE BACK

Words & Music by John Lennon & Paul McCartney.

E
A
to ⊕
Am
G6
FΔ7
I'll be back a-gain
'cause I
told you once be-fore good-bye
But
break my heart a-gain
This time
I will try to show that I'm
Not
I'll be back a-gain
2×, D.S.1×
2×, D.S.1×
E
A
1.
B
D.S.×
F#m
I came back a-gain
(1×) I love you so oh
I'm the one who
try-ing to pre-tend
(D.S.×) I wan-na go
but I hate to
2×
2×

Bm
E
D
E
D
E
wants you
Yes I'm the one who wants you oh ho
oh ho oh
leave you
You know I hate to leave you oh ho
oh ho oh
2.
A
C
Bm
C#m
I
through that you would re-al-ise
That if I

F#m
B7
D
E
D
E
D
E
run a-way from you that you would want me to But I got a big sur-prise Oh ho Oh ho Oh
D.S.
Coda
A
Am
A
Fade Out

I'LL CRY INSTEAD

Words & Music by John Lennon & Paul McCartney.

G
Am7
D
D.S. 1x D.S. 2x
'Cause I've just lost the on - ly girl I had
I can't talk to peo - ple than I meet
I'm gon - na break their hearts all 'round the world
2x. D.S.1x
2x
D7
C7
D.S.1X
D.S.2X
If I could get my way I'd
If I could see you now I'd
Yes I'm gon - na break them in two And
(Arpeggio)
(Arpeggio)
2x. D.S.1x
2x

C7
2x. D.S.1x D.S.2x
G
Am7
D
D7
get my - self locked up to - day but I can't So I'll cry in - stead
try to make you sad if some - how but I can't So I'll cry in - stead
show you what your lov - in' man can do Un - til then I'll cry in - stead
Arp.
1x, 2x, D.S.1X
to
1.
2.
B Bm
I've got a
Don't want to cry when there's peo - ple there
(Arpeggio)
D.S.1x
D.S.2x

Bm
A7
D
I get shy when they start to stare
I'm gon-na hide my-self a-way
Em
A7
D7
ay-hay
But I'll come back a-gain some-day
And when I
Arp.
D.S. 1×
Coda
G
D.S. 1. 2. al Coda

I'LL FOLLOW THE SUN

Words & Music by John Lennon & Paul McCartney.

D
C
C/B
D
G
1.
C
F
C
For to - mor-row may rain, so I'll fol-low the sun
But to - mor-row may rain, so I'll fol-low the
2.
C
C7
B
Dm
Fm6
C
sun
And now the time, has come, and so, my love, I must go

C7
Dm
Fm6
C
Dm
And through I lose a friend
In the end you will know
Oh
C
G7
F7
C
D
C
C/B
D
G
To Coda
One day you'll find
that I have gone
But to-morrow may rain so
I'll fol-low the

D
C
F
C
G7
F7
C
D
sun
But to-
C
C/B
D
G
C
C7
-mor-row may rain so I'll fol-low the sun And now the
Coda
C
FΔ7
C
sun
D.S.

I'LL GET YOU

Words & Music by John Lennon & Paul McCartney.

A
D♭
G♭
A♭7
D♭
-ag - ine I'm in love with you it's eas - y 'cause I know; I've im-ag - ined I'm in
think a-bout you night and day, I need you and it's true; When I think a - bout you
B♭m
G♭
A♭7
D♭
A♭m
love with you many, many, many times before. It's not like me to pre-tend, But I'll
I can say I'm nev-er, nev-er, nev-er ne - ver blue. So I'm tell - ing you, my friend, That I'll
T
A
B

D♭
B♭m
G♭
A♭7
to ⊕
D♭
get you. I'll get you in the end; Yes, I will, I'll get you in the end. Oh yeah, oh
1.
A♭
2.
A♭
B
G♭
D♭
yeah I yeah Well, there's gon - na be a time When I'm gon - na change your

D♭
E♭7
A♭7
mind. So you might as well re-sign your-self to me. Oh yeah, I'm
D.S.
Coda
D♭
A♭
D♭
A♭
D♭
yeah, oh yeah, oh yeah oh yeah, oh yeah.

I'M A LOSER

Words & Music by John Lennon & Paul McCartney.

FΔ7 D
B G D Fadd9 G
to be
Of all the love I have won or have lost
Al - though I laugh and I act like a clown
What have I done To de - serve such a fate
(H.H.)
G D Fadd9 G
B' G
there is one love I should ne - ver have crossed
Be - neath this mask I am wear - ing a frown.
I re - a - lize I have left it too late.
She was a girl
My tears are
And so it's true

D
Fadd9
G
D
in a mill - on, my friend
fall - ing Like rain from the sky
Pride comes be - fore a fall
I should have known She would
Is it for her Or my -
I'm tell - ing you So that
Fadd9
G
C
Am
D
Am
win in the end.
- self that I cry.
you won't lose all.
I'm A Los - er
And I lost some - one who's near
(Cym.)

D
G
Em
Am
F
D
to me I'm A Los - - - - er
and I'm not what I ap-pear to be
Harmonica
Fadd 9
(Cym.)

D.S.
(Fade Out at E)

I'M DOWN

Words & Music by John Lennon & Paul McCartney.

C
I'm real - ly down
G
Down on the ground.
I'm down.
3. (A ba-by I'm down.)
I'm down.
C
I'm real - ly down.
D7
G
How can you laugh when you know I'm down?
T
A
B

D7
G
How can you laugh
when you know I'm down
1.
2.
know I'm down ?
B
Wow !
C
G
T.C.

G
D7
G
Tr. Arm.
Tr. Arm.
D.C.
Coda
C
G
know I'm down? Woo!

C
G
D7
gliss.
C
G
(D7)
D
G
I'm real-ly down
A-baby you know I'm down,
I guess I'm down

G
I'm real-ly down
I'm down on the ground.
C
I'm real-ly down
I'm down.
G
I'm real-ly down
D7
Ah
Ah, ba-by I'm up-side down.
C
Ah
G
Ah
Oh yeah, yeah, yeah, yeah,
(D7)
Ah
yeah, I'm down,
Repeat & Fade Out

I ME MINE

Words & Music by George Harrison.

G
E
Am
Am
D7
G
E7
I, me, mine, I, me, mine
I, me, mine, I me mine
All through the night
E - ven those tears
I, me, mine, I, me, mine, I, me, mine
I, me, mine, I, me, mine, I, me, mine
(A. Guitar)
(A. Guitar)
Am
B
Dm
E7(b9)
Now they're fright-ened of leav-ing it Every-one's read-ing it com-in' on strong all the time
No one's fright-ened of play-ing it Every-one's say-ing it Flow-ing more free-ly than wine

1. 2.
Am
AmΔ7
Am7
Am6
FΔ7
C
All
through the day
I, me, mine
I, me, me, mine.
gliss.
(A. Guitar)
(E. Guitar)
Dm

Dm
Am
E7
I, me, me, mine,
gliss.
gliss.
E7
3.
Am
AmΔ7
Am7
Am6
FΔ7
All through the life I, me, mine
gliss.
(A. Guitar)

I'M HAPPY JUST TO DANCE WITH YOU

Words & Music by John Lennon & Paul McCartney.

B
1. (Straight)
2.
F#m G#7 A6 B6 E6 B7 E G#m
love you too I'm so hap-py when you dance with me
I don't (1X) wan-na kiss or hold your hand
(2X) need to hug or hold you tight
(D.S.1X / D.S.2X) - bo-dy tries to take my place
F#m B7 E G#m F#m B7 A A6/C#
If it's fun-ny try and un-der-stand
I just wan-na dance with you all night
Let's pre-tend we just can't see his face
There is real-ly noth-ing else I'd rath-er
In this world there's noth-ing I would rath-er
In this world there's noth-ing I would rath-er
(Bass Tom)

1.
2.
E
C#m
A
B7aug
to
E6
B7
E6
do
'Cos I'm hap-py just to dance with
you
I don't
you
just to
do
'Cos I'm hap-py just to dance with
do
(D.S.1X) 'Cos I'm hap-py just to dance with
(D.S.2X) I've dis - cov-ered I'm in love with
D.S.1X
C
C#m
F#m
G#7
C#m
F#m
G#7
C#m
dance with you
Is ev' - ry - thing I need
Be-fore this dance is through I think I'll
dance with you
oh
oh
oh
oh
oh
D.S.1X

Coda
F#m G#7 A6 B6 E6 B7
C#m F#m G#7
love you too ___ I'm so hap-py when you dance with me If some-
you 'Cos I'm
oh oh ___ oh oh ___ oh
oh oh ___
D.S.1x
D.S. 1. 2. (al Coda)
A B7aug C#m F#m G#7 A6 B6 E6
hap-py just to dance with you
oh oh ___ oh oh ___ oh

I'M LOOKING THROUGH YOU

Words & Music by John Lennon & Paul McCartney.

A
1.
2.
A♭
D♭
A♭/C
B♭m
Fm7
E♭
I'm look-ing (1x, 4x) through you
(2x) mov - ing
(3x) of me
Where did you go
I can - not hear
The some old way
I thought I
Your voice is
You were a -
3 x only
Mute
(Tambourine)
1 x Tacet
knew you
sooth - ing
- bove me
What did I know
But the words aren't clear
But not to - day
B
B♭m7
You don't look dif - ferent But
You don't sound dif - ferent I've
The on - ly dif - frence Is

to ⊕ (D.S.2 only)
A♭
D♭
E♭
A♭
D♭
A♭/C
B♭m
D♭
you have changed
learned the game
you're down there
I'm look-ing through you
I'm look-ing through you
I'm look-ing through you
You're not the same
You're not the same
And you're no-where
2 x only
A♭
1.
2.3.
A♭
Your lips are
(Tambourine)

C
D♭
A♭
D♭
Why, tell me why Did you not treat me right
Love has a nas-
E♭sus4
E♭
A♭
D♭
A♭/C
- ty ha - bit Of dis-ap - pear - ing o-ver - night
(2x) You're think-ing
(3x) I'm look-ing
Coda
You're not the same
D.S. 1. (2x)
D.S. 2. (3x)

D
Ab
Yeah,
Oh, ba - by you've changed
Aah,
I'm look-ing through you
Yeah,
I'm look-ing through you
You've changed
You've changed
You've changed
You've changed
Fade Out

I'M ONLY SLEEPING

Words & Music by John Lennon & Paul McCartney.

E♭m
A♭m
G♭
B
When I'm in the mid - dle of a dream
Run - ning ev - e - ry - where at such a speed
Stay in bed
Till they find
float up stream
There's no need
2 x only
B
Please don't wake me No, don't shake me Leave me where I am
(2.3.) Please don't spoil my day I'm miles a way And af - ter all
B♭m
Woo Woo Woo
Woo
D.S. time only

A♭m
to Φ 2.
B∆7
to Φ 1.
1.
2.
B∆7
E♭m
I'm on - ly sleep - ing
sleep - ing
C
D♭m
E♭7
A♭m
A♭m7
D♭m
Keep - ing an eye on the world go - ing by my win - dow
Tak - ing my time
Keep ing an eye on the world go ing by my win - dow

E♭7
A♭m
G♭
B
G♭
B♭7
D
E♭m
Lying there and star-ing at the ceil - ing
Wait - ing for a slee - py feel - ing
B.G. Simile~
(Reverse Elec. Guitar)
A♭m
G♭
B
G♭
B

D.S.

Coda 1.
BΔ7
E♭m
E
D♭m
Keep - ing an eye on the world
Keep - ing an eye on the world
T
A
B
1 2 3
E♭7
A♭m
A♭m7
D♭m
going by my win - dow
Tak - ing my time (When)
go-ing by my win - dow
D.C.

Coda 2.
B△7
F Tempo Rubato
E♭m
sleep - ing
sleep - ing
Q.C
H P
(B.G)
(E.G.)
S
Fade Out

I'M SO TIRED

Words & Music by John Lennon & Paul McCartney.

1.
A
Eaug
F#m
Dm
won - der should I get up and fix my - self a drink No no no I'm
2.
A
Eaug
won - der should I call you but I
curse Sir Wal-ter Ral - cigh He was
(Organ)
F#m
Dm
Know what you'd do
such a stu - pid get
B
A
You'd say I'm put-ting you on But it's no joke it's do-ing me harm you know I
(Org.)
(Piano)
2x
Dubbing Snare Dr.
1x
D.S.x

E
D
to Coda
A
can't sleep I can't stop my brain_You know it's three weeks I'm go-ing in-sane_You know I'd give you ev-ery-thing I've got for a little peace of mind___ I'm
Piano
D.S.
Coda
give you ev-ery-thing I've got for a little peace of mind___
give you ev-ery-thing I've got for a little peace of mind___ (talking)
(Piano)
8va
(Dubbing S.D.)

I NEED YOU

Words & Music by George Harrison.

Aadd9
Asus4
A
A
D
A
A7
Asus4
— you — Love you all the time — and ne - ver leave — you —
— me — How was I to know — you would — up - set — me —
— you — I could ne - ver real - ly live — with - out — you —
D.S.2x
2x D.S.1x D.S.2x
A
B
F♯m
C♯m
F♯m
Bm
A
Please come on back — to me — I'm lone-ly as — can be — I need —
I did-n't re - al-ize — As I looked in — your eyes — You told —
So come on back — and see — Just what you mean — to me — I need —
AH —
AH —
I need —
You told —
I need —
D.S.1x
2x D.S.1x

to Φ
1.
2.
C
A Aadd9
A
A
D
E
you
me
you
Oh yes you told me
You don't want my lov-in' an-y-more
AH
2x
cowbell
A
D
E
B7
That's when it hurt me
And feel-ing like this
I just can't go on an-y-
AH
AH
D.S.1x

Coda
E
- more
A
F#m
I need you
I need you
D.S.1x
D.S. 1.
2. al Coda
D
A
Aadd9
Asus4 A
I need you
I need you

IN MY LIFE

Words & Music by John Lennon & Paul McCartney.

F#m A7/G D Dm A A E
Woo Woo Woo
- mem-ber All my life though some have changed Some for - e - ver not for
lo - vers There is no one com - pares with you And these memo - ries lose their
F#m A7/G D Dm A
Woo Woo Woo
B F#m
be - tter Some have gone and some re - main All these (1.) pla - ces had their
mean - ing When I think of love as some - thing new Though I (2.3.) know I'll ne - ver lose af -
H.H. T.C.
(Tambourine)

D
G
A
F#m
mo-ments With lo-vers and friends I still can re-call Some are dead and some are
-fec-tion For peo-ple and things that went be-fore I know I'll of-ten stop and think a-
B
Dm7
to ⊕ 1.
A
E
liv-ing In my life I've loved them all But of
-bout them In my life I

2.
C
A
A
E
F#m
A7/G
D
Dm
love you more
8va bassa
8va bassa
T.C.
H.H.
A
A
E
F#m
A7/G
D
Dm

Coda
D
A
E
Dm7
(N.C.)
a tempo
Though I
love you more
In
my life I love you more
H
H.H.
T.C.
D.S.

THE INNER LIGHT

Words & Music by George Harrison.

E♭
With-
tr. tr. tr.
P H P H
A
E♭ E♭7 Fm7/E♭ E♭ E♭7 A♭/E♭ E♭ E♭7
- out go-ing out of my door I can know all things on earth With-out look-ing out of my
- out go-ing out of my door You can know all things on earth With-out look-ing out of my
P

Fm7
E♭
E♭
E♭7
A♭
E♭
A♭
E♭
E♭
E♭7
win - dow I could know the ways of heav - en
win - dow You can know the ways of heav - en
The far-ther one trav - els
the less one knows
The less one real - ly knows
Ar - rive with-out trav-el - ling
B
1 x Tacet
8va
mf
f

E♭
See all with-out look-ing do all with-out do-ing
1.
2.
E♭
With-
T
A
B
P H P H
2x

I SAW HER STANDING THERE

Words & Music by John Lennon & Paul McCartney.

E7
A7
E7
You know what I mean
And the way she looked Was way be-yond com-pare
and I I could see
That be-fore too long I'd fall in love with her
And we held each o-ther tight
And be-fore too long I fell in love with her
B7
B
E7
E7/G#
A7
C
So how could I dance with a-no-ther Oh when I
She would-n't dance with a-no-ther Oh when I
Now I'll ne-ver dance with a-no-ther Oh when I
4x (since I)

E7
B7
to ⊕ 1. 3.
E7
1.
2.
C
𝄋 2.
A7
saw her stand - ing there
saw her stand - ing there
saw her stand - ing
Well she
Well my heart went boom
When I crossed that room
And I held her hand
in mind
B7

B7
E7
to ⊕ 2.
⊕ Coda 1.
E7
B7
Oh we danced
there Ah
D.S. 1.
D
E7

E
B7
E7
A7
E7
B7
E7
B7
Well my
Coda 2.
A7
Oh
we danced
D.S. 2.
D.S. 3.

Coda 3.
E7
B7
E7
there
Oh since I
saw
her
stand
- ing there
B7
A7
E7
Yeah, well since I
saw
her
stand
-
ing
there

I SHOULD HAVE KNOWN BETTER

Words & Music by John Lennon & Paul McCartney.

G D G D G D G D
should have kno - wn bet - ter with a girl like you
should have re - al - ised a lot of things be - fore
That I would love ev' - ry - things that you do
If this is love you've got - ta give me more
Em C D G D
And I do
Give me more
Hey hey hey
Hey hey hey
And I do
Give me more

1.
G
D
B
Whoa whoa I
Ne-ver re-al-ised what a kiss could be
This could
on-ly hap-pen to me
Em
C
B7
C
Can't you see
Can't you see
That when I

C
G
B7
Em
tell you that I love ___ you ___ oh ___
You're gon - na say ___ you love me too ___
D.S.x
G
G7
C
D7
G
Hoo hoo hoo ___ Oh ___
And when I ask you to be mine ___

Em
C
D7
G
D
to
G
D
You're gon - na say you love me too
So oh
D.S.
2.
D
531

G
D
Em
C
D
G
D
T
A
B
1 2 3
Whoa whoa
Coda
You love me too
You love me too
D.S.
Repeat & Fade Out

IT'S ALL TOO MUCH

Words & Music by George Harrison.

A
C/G
(4times)
G
1X, 2X Tacet
Gadd9
G
C/G
G
Gadd9
It's all too mu - ch
G
B
G
(1x) When I look in - to your eyes your
(2x) Float - ing down the stream of time from
(D.S.1x) Sail me on a sil - ver sun where
D.S.1x
Feed Back
2X
8va
4X
(Top)
Synth &
Hand clap

G
love is there for me
life to life with me
I know that I'm free
And the more I go in - side the
Makes no dif-f'rence where you are or
Show me that I'm ev - 'ry - where and
Noise
D.S.1X
2X
(Tambourine)
more there is to see
where you'd like to be
get me home for tea
%2. C
C G
(Upper part 1X 2X Tacet)
G
Gadd 9
G
It's (1X D.S.2X) all too much for me to take the
It's (2X) all too much for me to take the
It's (D.S.1X) all too much for me to see the
D.S.2X
1X 2X Tacet
(Synth & Hand Clap)
Tambourine same pattern

C/G
G
Gadd9
G
love that's shin - ing all a - round you
love that's shin - ing all a - round you
love that's shin - ing all a - round you
Ev - 'ry - where it's what you make for
All the world is birth - day cake so
The more I learn The less I know and
D.S.2X
2X
us to take it's all too much
take a piece but not too
what I do it's all too
much
to Φ 1. 2.
1.
2.
8va

D
C/G
G
Gadd9
(4 times)
2X
(3X Tacet)
(4X Cutting C 1~4)
(1X, 2X Tacet)
4X
gliss.
(Synth & Hand Clap)
Feed Back
Coda 1.
much
It's
Coda 2.
D.S. 1.
D.S. 2.

E
C/G
1x Tacet
G
Gadd9
G
C/G
G
Gadd9
G
1x Tacet
It's too mu - ch
2x Tacet
(Ah)
T
A
B
10 11 12 13
10 11 12
10 11 12
1x Tacet
10 10 10 10 10 10 10 10
(Synth. & Hand Clap)
F
C/G
G
Gadd9
G
C/G
G
Gadd9
G
10 11 12
2x
2x
10 10 10 10 10 10 10 10

Repeat & Fade Out

IT'S ONLY LOVE

Words & Music by John Lennon & Paul McCartney.

B♭ F G Gaug C Em/B
I see you go by My oh my when you sigh my
you and I should flight Ev'-ry night just the sight of
(Guitar I) 1X, 2X
H
2X
1X, 2X
B♭ F G Gaug
B
F G
my in - side just flies Butter-flies why am I so shy when I'm be -
you make night - time bright Ve - ry bright have-n't I the right to make it

C
Am
B♭
G
C
-side you
up girl
It's on - ly love and that is all
Why should I feel the way I do
2x
(Tambourine)
Am
B♭
G
F
1.
G
It's on - ly love and that is all
But it's so hard lov-ing you
so hard lov-ing

2.
C
G
F
G
C
Am
you
Yes it's so hard
lov-ing
you
lov-ing
you
(with tremolo)
(Tambourine)
C
Am
C
Am
C

IT WON'T BE LONG

Words & Music by John Lennon & Paul McCartney.

C#m
A
A(b9)
E
E
B
E
D.S.x
long Yeh till I be - long to you
Ev - 'ry night when
Ev - 'ry night the
Ev - 'ry day
Yeh
Ah
h.c
C
E
D.S.x
C
E
ev - 'ry bo - dy has fun
tears come down from my eyes
we'll be hap - py I know
Here am I sit - ting all on my own
Ev - 'ry day I've done no - thing but cry
Now I know that you won't leave me no more
2x. D.S.x

E
C
C#m
D.S.
E
C#m
to
It won't be long Yeh Yeh Yeh
1.2.) It won't be long Yeh
D.S.) It won't be long
Yeh Yeh It won't be long Yeh till
D.S.x
Yeh Yeh Yeh Yeh Yeh Yeh Yeh
h.c
2x
2x D.S.x
A
A(b9)
E
D
E
D#aug
I be-long to you
Since you left me
I'm so a-lone Now you're
Ah
You left me I'm so a-
H.H. close
2x

D6
C#7
A
B7
F#m7
com-ing you're com-ing on home I'll be good like I know I should You're com-ing home you're com-ing
-lone Now you're co-ming on home I should com-ing on home
1.
2.
Coda
Slow
home home So
I be-long to you Woo
Ah woo
D.S.

I'VE GOT A FEELING

Words & Music by John Lennon & Paul McCartney.

A D/A A D/A A D/A A D/A A D/A
That's right. I've got a feel - ing a feel-ing I can't hide oh no — no — oh no oh no —
A7 E G D A D/A A D/A
yeah — yeah — I've got a feel - ing yeah

B
A
D/A
Oh please be-lieve_ me
I'd hate to miss_ the train
oh yeah_ Yeah
oh yeah_
I've got a feel - ing
that keeps me on_ my toes
oh yeah_
oh yeah_
H
And if you leave_ me
I won't be late_ a-gain
oh no_
oh no_
oh no_
I've got a feel - ing
I think that every-body_ knows
oh yeah_
oh yeah_
oh yeah_
4

A7
E G D
A
D/A
A
D/A
yeah
yeah
I've got a feel - ing
yeah
I've got a feeling
yeah
yeah
I've got a feel - ing
yeah
yeah
C
1.
E
G7
D7
A7
All these years I've been wan-der-ing a-round won-der-ing how come no-bo-dy told me All that I was look-ing for was some-body who looked like you

D
2.
A7
A
D/A
Ev-'ry-bo-dy had a hard year
Ev-'ry-bo-dy had a good year,
Ev-'ry-bo-dy had a good time
Ev-'ry-bo-dy let their hair down
Ev-'ry-bo-dy had a wet dream
Ev-'ry-bo-dy pulled their socks up
vib.
hu hu hu hu hu hu
C D
H
E
1.
Ev-'ry-bo-dy saw the sun shine. oh yeah
Ev-'ry-bo-dy put their foot down, oh yeah
oh yeah
oh
yeah

A7
A
D/A
F
(1) I've got a feel-ing a feel-ing I can't hide oh no
(2) I've got a feel-ing a feel-ing deep in - side oh yeah
Ev-'ry-bo-dy had a good year
Ev-'ry-bo-dy had a good year
Ev-'ry-bo-dy had a hard time
Ev-'ry-bo-dy let their hair down
1.
oh yeah
Ev-'ry-bo-dy had a wet dream
Ev-'ry-bo-dy saw the sun shine
2.
oh no no
Ev-'ry-bo-dy pulled their socks up

A
D/A
A7
yeah
Ev-'ry-bo-dy put their foot down oh yeah
I've got a feel - ing
I've got a feel-
ing
Oh yeah
I've got a feel - ing
yeah
A

I'VE JUST SEEN A FACE

Words & Music by John Lennon & Paul McCartney.

D
E
1.(Straight)
2(Straight)
A
A
F#m
(1X, D.S.2X) I've just seen a face I can't for-get the time or place where we just met she's just the girl
(2X) Had it been an-oth-er day I might have looked the oth-er way and I'd have ne-ver been
(D.S.1X) I have ne-ver known the like of this I've been a-lone and I have missed things and kept out
(12 Strings Acoustic Guitar)
(Acoustic Guitar)
(Brush)
(Shaker)

F#m
D
E
for me and I want all the world to see we've met
a-ware but as it is I'll dream of her to-night
of sight for oth-er girls were ne-ver quite like this
Mm mm mm (1x) mm mm mm
La la la (D.S.2) La la la
Da da da (2x) la la la
(D.S.1) da da da
A
B E
D
A
Fall - ing Yes I am fall - ing And she keeps call - ing
D.S.2x
2x. D.S.1x D.S.2x
(shaker)

D
A
me back a-gain
to Φ 1. 2.
D.S.1x
D.S.2x
D.S. 1.
Φ Coda 1. C
A
Yeah
Pa Pa Pa Pa
(shaker)
F#m

D
E
A
D
E
Fall - ing
Yes I am
1 2 3
D
A
D
A
Fall - ing
And she keeps
call - ing
me back a-gain
D.S. 2

Coda 2
E
D
A
(1x) Fall - ing
(2x) oh Fall - ing
Yes I am Fall - ing
And she keeps call - ing
1x
(shaker)
2x
D
1.
A
2.
D
E
A
me back a - gain
1x

I WANNA BE YOUR MAN

Words & Music by John Lennon & Paul McCartney.

E7
2x
1.
2.
lo-ver ba - by I wan-na be your man
o-ther ba - by Like, no o-ther can
love me ba - by I wan-na be your man
I wan-na be your man
2x S
D.S.2 1x
D.S. 2x
1x only
D.S.1 1x
D.S.1x D.S.2x
B
F#7
B7
E
C#7
I wan-na be your man
I wan-na be your man
I wan-na be your
8va

E
D/E
to ⊕ 1.2.
⊕Coda 1.
C E7
man
wow
Ah
gliss.
gliss
P
C
U D
(H.H. Closed)
(H.H. Open)
D.S. 1.
Hey
No
Oh
Ah
Oh

E7
D.S. 2.
Coda 2.
D/E
D
E7
Wah
gliss
(H.H. Open)
I wan-na be your man oh I wan-na be your man oh I wan-na be your man Ho Ho
Fade Out

I WANT TO HOLD YOUR HAND

Words & Music by John Lennon & Paul McCartney.

A
G
D7
Em
B7
Em
G
I'll___ tell you some-thing___ I think you'll un - der - stand When I'll___ Say that
U. D.
T
A
B
D7
Em
B7
C
D7
G
Em
some-thing___ I WANT TO HOLD YOUR HAND___ I WANT TO HOLD YOUR HAND___
C

B
C
D7
G
Em
B7
I WANT TO HOLD YOUR HAND
Oh (1.) please
(2.3.) you
say to me
got that some - thing,
you'll let me be your
I think you'll un - der -
man,
stand.
and
When
please
I
say to me
say that some - thing,
D.S.X (feel)
you'll let me hold your hand.
I WANT TO HOLD YOUR HAND,
T
A
B

C
C D7 G Em to⊕ C D7 G
Upper Part 1x Tacet
Dm7
Now, let me hold your hand,
I WANT TO HOLD YOUR HAND,
I WANT TO HOLD YOUR HAND,
I WANT TO HOLD YOUR HAND,
and when I
G7 C Am Dm7 G7 C D
touch you, I feel hap-py in-side.
It's such a feel-ing that my love I can't hide,

1.
2.
D
C D
C D
D7
I can't hide,
I can't hide.
Yeah,
Yeah,
D.S.
Coda
C
D7
B7
G
I WANT TO HOLD YOUR HAND,
I WANT TO HOLD YOUR HAND.

I WANT TO TELL YOU

Words & Music by George Harrison.

A
B7
E7
A7
you
My head is filled with things to say
When you're here
All those words they seem to slip a - way
T
A
B

B
A
A
B7
(2.) When I get near you
(3.4.) I want to tell you
The games be - gin to drag me down
I feel hung up And I don't know why
1x only
E7
A7
to
It's all right
I don't mind,
I'll make you may - be next
I could wait for - ev - er
time a - round
I've got time

A7
C
Bm
Bdim
A
B7
But if I seem to act un - kind It's on - ly me, it's not my mind
Some-times I wish I knew you well Then I could speak my mind and tell you
Bm
Bdim
A
1.
2.
A
That is con - fus - ing things
May-be you'd un - der - stand
D.S.

Coda
A7
D
A7
I've got time
(Tambourine)
Ah
Ah
Ah
Ah
Ah
I've got time
Fade Out

I WANT YOU

Words & Music by John Lennon & Paul McCartney.

A
Am7
you
I want you so bad
I want you
1x only
C
D
P
h.c
UD
2x
2x Dr.'s
1x only Dr's
Simile
Am7
C
D
F
G
E7-9
Am7
I want you so bad
It's driv-ing me mad
It's driv-ing me mad
1x only
hUD P
1x tacet
Cym.

A7
Dm7
I want you
I want you so bad babe
I want
you
I want you so bad
Dm7
F
C
B♭
(N.C.)
It's driv-ing me mad It's driv - ing me
1 x only

E7-9
mad
1.
2.
B
Dm
Dm
F
I want
She's so
(H.H)
(H.H)

E7-9
D.S. time only
B♭7
Aaug7
Dm
Dm/F
hea-vy
hea - vy, hea - vy,
hea-vy
hea - vy
C
VOCAL D.S. x only
Am7
I want you
I want you so
1 x play Ad-lib.
(D.S. x Simile)
h.c
C D
h.c D P
Mute
H

Am7
bad I want you I want you so bad It's
Am7 C
D F G E7-9 Am7 A7 Dm7
driv-ing me mad It's driv-ing me mad I want you

Dm7
You know I want you so bad babe
I want you
You know I want you so
Dm7
F
C
Bb
(N.C.)
E7-9
bad It's driv-ing me mad It's driv-ing me mad
Yeah

E7-9
to Φ
Φ Coda
She's so
She's so
(H.H)
(H.H)
D.S.
D
Dm
Dm/F
E7-9
B♭7
1～14
Aaug7
15
Aaug7
Noise (3x)→
8va bassa
(Tuning)
Cym.

I WILL

Words & Music by John Lennon & Paul McCartney.

D.S.x(Dm B♭ F)
B♭ C7 F B♭ C7 to⊕ 1. F Dm
a lone - ly life - time If you want me to I will
- ver real - ly mat - tered I will al - ways feel the same
so I can hear you Make it ea - sy to be near
D.S.x
(Arpeggio)
Gm7 C7 2. F F7 B B♭ Am Dm Gm7 C7
For if Love you for e - ver and for - e - ver Love you with all my heart
(shaker)
(Bongo)

F
F7
B♭
Am
Dm
G7
C7
Love you when-e - ver we're to-ge - ther
Love you when we're a - part
And when
D.S.
Coda
Dm
B♭
F
B♭
C7
Dm
B♭
F
Fdim
you
For the things you do
en-dear you to me
And

Gm
C7
C
D♭7
F
you know
I will
I will
F7
B♭
Am
Dm
Gm7
C7
F
Ooo
la
T
A
B

JULIA

Words & Music by John Lennon & Paul McCartney.

G7add9 Gm D Bm7 F#m A
to Coda 1. 2. D
calls me So I sing a song of love Ju - li -
calls me So I sing a song of love Ju - li - a
touch me So I sing a song of love Ju - li -
touch me So I sing a song of love Ju - li -
F7add9 Fm C Am7 Em G C
C
C#m D Bm7 Bm6 F#m7 F#m6
Her hair of float-ing sky is shim-mer-ing glim-mer-ing In the sun
Bm C Am7 Am6 Em7 Em6
F#m+5 F#m
Em+5 Em
D.S. 1.
Coda 1.
D
- a
D
D Bm7
When I can-not sing my heart
C C Am7

Coda 2.
F#m
D
Bm7
A
I can on - ly speak my mind Ju - li - a
Em
C
Am7
G
D.S. 2.
E
Am7
Am9
B7
G7add9
Gm
Hum
calls me
So I sing a song of love for
Gm7
Gm9
A7
F7add9
Fm
Ju - li - a Ju - li - a Ju - li - a
DΔ7
CΔ7

KANSAS CITY

Words & Music by Jerry Leiber & Mike Stoller.

A
G
G7
___, Kan - sas ci - ty
coming to get my baby back home___
yeah, yeah___,
I'm gon-
C
G
- na Kan - sas ci - ty
coming to get my baby back home___
yeah, yeah___,
Well, it's a

D
C
G
G C C# D
long, long time___, since my ba - by's been gone___ Ah___
B
G
G7
___, Kan- sas ci - ty coming to get my baby on time___ yeah, yeah___, I'm gon -

C
G
D
- na Kan-sas ci - ty
coming to get my ba - by on ___ time ___
yeah, yeah ___ ,
It's just a one, two, three ___ four,
T
A
B
C
G
G C C♯D
C
G
five, six, se - ven, eight, nine
Wah ___ !
c
p

G
G7
C
G
D
C
G
continue to
"Hey, Hey, Hey"

A
G
Hey, hey, hey, hey
Hey, ba - by
G7
Hey, hey, hey, hey
Hey, ba - by
you're no clown
C
You're no clown
G
You're no clown
D
I say you're no clown.
Now, now, now, now Tell me ba - by

C
G
1.
2.
G C C# D
what's been wrong with you
Hey, hey, hey,
Well, I'll say bye
B
G
bye, bye, bye, bye, bye, bye, bye, bye, bye, bye, bye bye
G7
bye, bye, ba-by bye, bye,
Oh, so long

C
bye, bye
bye, bye
bye, bye
G
bye, bye
bye, bye
bye, bye
Bye, bye, ba - by I'm
gone
Yeah,
I said
D
C
G
G C C# D
bye,
bye
ba - by
bye
bye
bye
bye
bye, bye
Repeat & Fade Out

LADY MADONNA

Words & Music by John Lennon & Paul McCartney.

to Φ 2.
B
A D A D F G A A D A D
child-ren at__ your feet
Won-der how you man-age to make __ ends meet__
(1x) Who finds _ the mo - ney
When you pay the rent__
T
A
B
0 0 3 4 0 0 2 2
3 3 5 5 7 7 7 7
S
A D F G A
(DS1x Chorus)
𝄋 1. Dm7
C
Pa pa pa pa__ pa pa
G7
pa pa pa
Did you think that mo-ney was__
hea - ven sent ?__
(1x) Fri - day night__ ar - rives__ with-out__ a suit - case
(DS1x) Tues - day__ af - ter-noon__ is__ ne - ver end - ing
5 5 3 3 2 2 5 5

C
Am7
Dm7
G7
pa pa pa pa pa pa pa pa pa pa pa pa pa pa pa pa pa pa pa pa pa pa
to ⊕ 1.
C
Bm7
Sun-day mor-ning creep-ing like a nun
Mon-day's child has learned to tie his boot - legs
See how they
Wednes-day mor-ning pa-pers did-n't come
Thurs-day night your stock-ing need-ed mend - ing
1x Crush
(Ride Cym.)
E7sus4
E7
D
A
D
A
D
A
D
F
G
A
run
(1x) La-dy Ma-don-na
ba-by at your breast
Won-ders how you man-age to feed the rest
(2x) La-dy Ma-don-na
ly-ing on the bed
Lis-ten to the mu-sic play-ing in your head

E
A D A D A D A D
1.
F G A
F
Dm7
(Upper Chorus)
Pa pa pa pa pa pa
(Lower Chorus)
pa pa pa pa
G7 pa pa pa
pa
C pa pa pa pa pa pa
pa pa pa pa
Am7
pa pa pa pa pa
pa
Dm7
pa pa pa pa pa pa
pa pa pa pa
T
A
B

G7
pa pa pa
pa
C
Bm7
E7sus4
E7
See how they run
2.
F G A
Coda 1.
E7sus4 E7
run
(Ride Cym.)
D.S. 1.
(Ride Cym)
D.S. 2.
Coda 2.
F G A G/B Cm G/B A
ends meet
A G/B
Cm G/B A
H.C
H.C

LET IT BE

Words & Music by John Lennon & Paul McCartney.

1.
2.
B
Am F△7 F6 C G F C F G Am C/G
Mother Ma - ry comes to me
Standing right in front of me
S - peak-ing words of wis - dom, let it be
And
Let it be let it be let it be
(Organ.)
8va
T
A
B
F C C G F C
C
C G
let it be
Whis-per words of wis-dom
let it be
And
when the bro - ken heart - ed peo - ple
when the night is cloud - y There is
(2x only Organ.)
1x tacet
1x tacet.
1x tacet

Am F△7 F6 C G F C C G
Liv-ing in the world a-gree There will be (an)an-swer let it be For though they may- be part-ed there is
still a light that shines on me Shine un-till to-mor - row let it be I wake up to the sound of mu-sic
2x only
2x only
Am F C G F C D Am C/G
still a chance that they will see There will be (an)ans-wer let it be
Moth-er Ma - ry comes to me Speak-ing words of wis-dom let it be
Let it be let it be let it be
2x
8va.
1x tacet.

E
F C C G F G Am C/G F C
let it be
yeah There will be (an) ans-wer let it be
There will be (an) ans-wer let it be
Let it be let it be let it be let it be
Let it be let it be let it be yeah let it be
(Organ.)
8va.
(Brass)
2x only
C G F C F C/E G7/D C Bb F/A G F C F C
Whis-per words of wis-dom let it be
There will be (an) ans-wer let it be
1.
F
(E. Piano)
(Organ)
8va. bassa

G
C G Am F C G F C
8va.
S H C UD
P S H
C G Am F C G F C
H
Am C/G
Let it be let it be yeah let it be
(Organ)
8va.
4
UD P UD PH
S

2.
I
F
C
G
Am
C/G
yeah let it be
Whis-per words of wis-dom let it be
And
Let it be
let it be
let it be
(Brass.)
H
S
UD
C
T
A
B
F
C
G
yeah let it be
Whis-per words of wis-dom let it be
C/E
G7/D
Bb
F/A
(Brass.)
(E.Piano)

LITTLE CHILD

Words & Music by John Lennon & Paul McCartney.

E7
E7
A
E7
B7
A
Lit-tle Child won't you dance with me
I'm so sad and lone - ly
tr.
tr.
1.
F#7
B7
2.
F#7
B7
E
B
E
Ba - by take a chance with me
Lit-tle Child. Ba - by take a chance with me
If you want some - one to make you
by my side you're the
1x only
T
A
B

B7
E
F#7
B7
feel so fine___ Then we'll have some fun when you're mine, all mine___ So come on come on___ come on___ Lit-tle Child_
on - ly one___ Don't you run and hide Just come on come on___ So come on come on___ come on___ Lit-tle Child_
D.S.x
T
A
B
D.S.x
C
E7
E7
A
E7
B7
(1. D.S.) Lit-tle Child___ Lit-tle Child___ won't you dance with me___ I'm___ so sad and
D.S.x
D.S.x
D.S.x

A
F#7
B7
to ⊕
E
D E7
tone - ly
Ba - by take a chance with me
wow
tr.
A
E7

E7
B7
A
F#7
B7
When you're
tr.
3
T
A
B
7 8 9
5 6 7
2 3 4
2 3 4
D.S.
Coda
E
C#7
F#7
B7
E
C#7
F#7
B7
E
C#7
oh yeah
Ba - by take a chance with me
oh yeah
Ba - by take a chance with me
oh yeah
1 2 3
2 3 4
Fade Out

THE LONG AND WINDING ROAD

Words & Music by John Lennon & Paul McCartney.

Cm
Fm
B♭7
D♭/E♭
A♭
Gm
Cm
Fm
B♭7
- pear
I've seen that road be-fore
It al-ways leads me here.
lead me to your door
(Chorus)
E♭
B
Cm
A♭/B♭
E♭
E♭7
A♭
The (1.) wild and wind-y night that the rain washed a - way
(2.3.) still they lead me back to the long wind-ing road
1X omit
2X, 3X
(Horns)
8va
T
A
B

A♭ Gm Cm Fm B♭7 D♭/E♭ A♭ Gm
has left a pool of tears crying for the day Why leave me stand-
You left me stand - ing here a long long time a-go Don't leave me wait-
Cm Fm B♭7 E♭
- ing here, let me know the way
- ing here, lead me to your door
C 1.
E♭/B♭ A♭ E♭/G Fm B♭7
Many times I've been alone and many times I've cried
T
A
B

2.
E♭/B♭
A♭
Fm
B♭7
E♭/G
An-y-way you'll nev-er know the man-y ways I've tried but
(Strings)→
T
A
B
Coda
E♭
A♭/B♭
I
lead me to your door Yeah yeah yeah yeah
D.S.

LONG LONG LONG

Words & Music by George Harrison.

Gm
F
Gm/B♭
C
long time
long time
be you
How could I ever have lost you
Now I'm so hap-py I found you
How can I ever mis-place you
Em
D
G
A
T
A
B
2×
When I loved you
How I love you
How I want you
C7
It took a
A7
D.S.x

C7
B
B♭
F
C
Gm
Gm
So ma-ny tears I was sear - ch-ing
A7
G
D
A
Em
Em
1 2 3
(Top)
B♭
F
C
Gm
B♭
C
C
So ma - ny tears I was wast - ing oh oh
Now I can
G
D
A
Em
G
A
A
D.S.

Coda
C
Gm
F
C
Gm
F
C
Gm
oh I
love
you
You know that I
need
you
Ooh
I
Em
D
A
Em
D
A
Em
T
A
B
1 2 3
F
C
C
(Slow)
N.C.
love
you
AH
D
A
A
Roll

LONG TALL SALLY

Words & Music by Enotris Johnson, Richard Penniman & Robert Blackwell.

C
G
D7
- by,
- by,
- by,
yeah, now ba - by,
Woo ba - by,
C7
G
to
1.
D7
2.
D7
B
G
some fun to-night
I
D.S.x only
C D U D U
C D U D U
S
S
T
A
B

G
C
G
D7
C7
G

D7
Well
D.S.
Coda
D7
C
G
C
G

G
D7
C7
G
D7
Well we're gon-na
Q.C
h.U D
C
C
D
Q.C
h.U D
C
C
D
S
S
S
S
D
G
C
have some fun to-night, have some fun to-night Ev-'ry-thing's all right,-

C
G
D7
C7
have some fun to-night, Have some fun, yeah, yeah,
G
D7
E
G
yeah, (woo) We're gon-na have some fun to-night, have some fun to-night,

G
C
G
E - v - 'ry-thing's all right,
have some fun to-night,
Yeah, we'll have
D7
C7
G
G9
some fun,
some fun to-night.

LOVELY RITA

Words & Music by John Lennon & Paul McCartney.

A♭
E♭
B♭
B
E♭
D♭
A♭
E♭
B♭
Love-ly Ri-ta me-ter maid__ no-thing can come be-tween us
me-ter maid__ Love-ly Ri-ta__ me-ter maid__
Cm
F
B♭
C
E♭
A♭
D♭
G♭
When it gets dark I tow your heart a-way
Stand-ing by a park-ing me-ter when I caught a glimpse of Ri-ta
Took her out and tried to win__ her had a laugh and o-ver din-ner

E♭ B♭ E♭ A♭ D♭ G♭
Fill-ing in a tick-et in her lit-tle white book
Told her I would real-ly like to see her a - gain
In a cap she looked much old - er
Got the bill and Ri-ta paid__ it
And the bag a-cross her should - er
Took her home and near-ly made__ it
chi-k chi-k chi-k chi-k chi-k chi-k chi-k
E♭ B♭ E♭ Cm Fm B♭ D E♭ D♭ A♭
made her look a lit-tle like a mil-i-t'ry man__
sit-ting on a so-fa with a sis-ter or two__
Love-ly Ri-ta me-ter maid__
2x (oh__)
chi-k chi-k chi-k chi-k chi-k chi-k chi-k

E♭ B♭ Cm F
1.
B♭
may I in - quire dis - creet - ly when are you free to take some tea with me
where would I be with - out you give us a wink and make me think of
2x Tacet
Love - ly Ri - ta Love - ly me - ter maid
B♭sus4 B♭
E
E♭ D♭ A♭ E♭ B♭ Cm F
Ri - ta
Ah
Piano Solo

2.
B♭
A♭
E♭
B♭
you Love-ly me-ter maid Ri-ta me-ter maid
Love - ly Ri - ta me-ter maid__ Love - ly Ri - ta__ me-ter maid__
gliss.
oh, Love-ly Ri-ta me-ter, me-ter maid La, la, la, la, la, la, la, la, la,
Love - ly Ri - ta__ me-ter maid__ Love - ly Ri - ta__ me-ter maid__ Ha__ Ha__
F
A♭m

A♭m
la. la, la, la, la, la, la, la, la, la, la, ho___ oh ah ah ah ah
Ha– Ha– Ha– Ha– Ha, Ha, Ha, Ha, Ha, Ha, Ha___ oo Ah ah
ah ah ah ah ah ah ah
Ha, Ha, Ha, Ha Ha, Ha, Ah
gliss.

LOVE ME DO

Words & Music by John Lennon & Paul McCartney.

A 𝄋1. 2. (Straight)
C
G
G
C
Love
Love
me do
You
G
C
G
C
know
I
love you
I'll
al
-
ways
be true
So
please

C
G
C
G
to Φ 1. 2.
Love me do
oh love me do
1 2 3
1.
C
2.
G
B
D
C
Some one to love
Some - bo - dy

G
D
C
G
new
Some - one to love
Some - one like you
D.S. 1.
Coda 1.
C
G
D
C
G
D

D
C
G
4.
T
A
B
1 2 3
Coda 2.
C
G
C
G
Yeah
Love
me
do
oh
love me
do
3
5
D.S. 2.
Fade Out

LOVE YOU TO

Words & Music by George Harrison.

N.C.
Harm.
Harm.
Harm.
Tempo giusto
C
A C
Each day just goes so fast I turn a - round, it's past
time is so short A new one can't be bought
- ple stand - ing round Who'll screw you in the ground

C
You don't get time to hang a sign on me
But what you've got means such a lot to me
They'll fill you in with all their sins, you'll see
B Bb C Bb C Bb C Bb
Love me while you can
Make love all day long
I'll make love to you
Be - fore I'm a dead old man
Make love sing-ing songs
If you want me to
(Reverse)
T
A
B
To

C
1.
C
2.
C
A life

C
D
B♭
C
B♭
C
B♭
C
B♭
Make love all__ day long
Make love sing-ing songs
(Reverse)
There's peo -
D.S.
Coda
C
accel.

C

Fade Out

LUCY IN THE SKY WITH DIAMONDS

Words & Music by John Lennon & Paul McCartney.

A/F# A/F A A/G A/F# A/F
boat on a ri - ver with tan - ger - ine trees and mar - ma - lade skies
bridge by a fount - ain where rock - ing horse peo - ple eat marsh - mal - low pies
train in a sta - tion with plast - i - cine port - ers with look - ing glass ties
A A/G A/F# A/F A
Some - bo - dy calls you, you an - swer quite slow - ly a girl with kal -
Ev' - ry - one smiles as you drift past the flow - ers that grow so in -
Sud - den - ly some - one is there at the turn - stile the girl with kal -

A/G
A/F#
to Φ
Dm
Dm/C
B
B♭
-eid - o - scope eyes.
-cred - ib - ly high.
-eid - o - scope eyes.
Cel - lo - phane
News pa - per tax -
Slide Guitar
C
F
B♭
flow - ers of yel - low and green tow - er - ing o - ver your head
- is ap - pear on the shore wait - ing to take you a - way

C
G
D
C
(2x with chorus)
G
C
Look for the girl with the sun in her eyes and she's gone
Climb in the back with your head in the clouds and you're gone
Lu-cy in the sky with
(organ)
(Slide Guitar)
D
G
C
D
G
C
D
D
dia--monds, Lu-cy in the sky with dia--monds, Lu-cy in the sky with dia--monds, Ah
(Organ)

D.S.

Coda
Dm
D
G
C
D
Lu - cy in the sky with dia - - monds
Lu - cy in the sky with
(Organ)
dia - - monds
Lu - cy in the sky with dia - - monds
A
Ah
1 2 3
Repeat & Fade Out

MAGGIE MAE

Arranged by John Lennon, Paul McCartney,
George Harrison & Richard Starkey.

G
D7
G
nev - er walk down Lime Street an - y more
Oh, the judge she guilt - y found
C
D7
her of rob-bing the home - ward bound - er
that dir - ty no good rob-bin' Mag-gie Mae

G
B
C
G
It's the part of Liv- er - pool
She re - turned me to
D7
G
Ah
two pound ten a week that was my pay

MAGICAL MYSTERY TOUR

Words & Music by John Lennon & Paul McCartney.

E
A
E
G
A
step right this way !
(1x, 2x) Roll up
Roll up for the mys - te-ry tour
2X
Roll up
Roll up for the mys - te-ry tour
B
We've got ev -
And that's an

E
-'ry-thing you need
in - vi - ta - tion
G
A
Roll up for the mys - te - ry tour
2X(
x(
E
Sa - tis - fac - tion guar - an - teed
Roll up
To make a Re - ser - va - tion
4.
G
A
Roll up for the mys - te - ry tour
C
D
D/C
G/B
(1x) The ma - gi - cal mys - te - ry tour is wait - ing to take you a -
(2x) The ma - gi - cal mys - te - ry tour is hop - ing to take you a -

Gm/B♭
D/A
A
D
B
-way
Wait - ing to take you a - way
-way
Hop - ing to take you a - way
2X
1 2 3
2 3 4
F#m7
B
Mys - te - ry trip
roll

F#m7
G#m7
A
B
E
E
Ah
(Slow down)
roll
G
A
E
The ma - gi-cal mys - te-ry tour
Roll up

G
A
E
And that's an in - vi - ta - tion
G
Roll up for the mys - te-ry tour
Roll up
Roll up for the mys -
A
E
To make a re - ser-va - tion
G
A
- te-ry tour
Roll up
Roll up for the mys - te-ry tour

F
D
D/C
G/B
Gm/B♭
D/A
The ma - gi - cal mys - te - ry tour is com - ing to take you a - way
The ma gi cal mys te ry tour is dy - ing to take you a - way
Com - ing to take you a -
Dy - ing to take you a -
2x
1.
2.
A
A
D
- way
- way take you to - day
roll
roll
roll

D
G
Dm7
T
A
B
roll
Fade Out

MARTHA MY DEAR

Words & Music by John Lennon & Paul McCartney.

B♭7
A♭△7
B♭7
A♭△7
B♭
B♭7
A
E♭
E♭
D
Mar-tha __ my dear
though I spend __ my
Mar-tha __ my dear
you have al - ways
(Strings)
(Piano & Cello)
1 X Tacet
D.S.X
Gm
Gm/F
C7
F
B♭
A♭add 9
B♭7
A♭
B♭7
A♭
days in con-ver-sa - tion
please
Re-mem-ber
me
Mar-tha my __ love ___
Don't for-get __ me ___
Mar-tha my __ dear __
been my in-spi-ra - tion
please
Be good to
me
Mar-tha my __ love ___
Don't for-get __ me ___
Mar-tha my __ dear __
gliss.
gliss.

to Φ B
B♭ B♭7 Dm7 Gm9 F
Hold your head up you sil - ly girl look what you've done When you find
Hold your hand out you sil - ly girl see what you've done When you find
(2X Brass)
(I)
(II)
D.S.X
(Piano & Tuba)
1 X Tacet
(1X Tacet)
Csus4 C Csus4 C A7 Dm7 Gm9 Dm7
1.
C
your-self in the thick of it Help your-self to a bit of what is all a-round you Sil-ly girl Take a good looka -
your-self in the thick of it Help your-self to a bit of what is all a-round you Sil-ly girl
(Brass)
2X

G9
Dm7
G9
B♭△7
C
B♭△7
- round you___ Take a good ___ look you're bound to___ see___ That you and me___ were meant to be___ for each o -
Dm7
Gm9
E♭
D
E♭
E♭
D
- ther___ sil-ly girl___
(Trumpet)
(Trombone)
(Hand Clap)

Gm
Gm/F
C7
F
B♭
A♭Δ9
B♭7
A♭Δ7
B♭7
A♭Δ7
B♭
B♭7
2. Gm9
E♭
Coda
E♭
gliss.
D.S.

MATCHBOX

Words & Music by Carl Lee Perkins.

(with Repeat)
A
A7
(1.5.) sit-tin' here watch - in', match - box hole in my clothes; I said I'm
(2.) poor boy and I'm a long way from home; I'm an ol'
(3.) want my peach-es hon-ey please don't shake my tree; If you
(4.) your lit-tle dog till your big dog comes; Let me be
D7
A7
sit-tin' here won - d'rin', (watch - in') match - box hole in my clothes. I
poor boy and I'm a long way from home; I've
don't want any of those peach-es, hon-ey, please don't mess a - round my tree. I got news
your lit-tle dog till your big dog comes, And when your
T A B

A7
E7
to Φ
A7
1. 2.
E7
3.
E7
ain't got no match - es, but I sure got a long___ way to go.___
ne - ver been hap - py, 'cause ev - 'ry - thing I ev - er did was wrong.
for you ba - by, leave me here in___ mis - er - y.___ (Spoken) All right!
big dog gets___ here, watch how your pup - py dog runs.
I'm an ol'
Well,___ if you don't
Well,___ I said I'm
B
A7
D7
QC
HUD
H P

D7
A7
E7
D7
QC
S
H P
C
UD
A7
Well ___ let me be_
Coda
A7
A♭
D.S.

MAXWELL'S SILVER HAMMER

Words & Music by John Lennon & Paul McCartney.

A7 D A7 D D/C# B7
— With a test- tube— Oh, oh, oh,— oh.— Max- well E- di-son ma- jor-ing in me- di- cine,
— an un-pleas- ant— sce - e - e- ene.— She tells Max to stay When the class has gone a- way,
- i-al pic - tures,— Oh, oh, oh,— oh.— Rose and Val- er- ie scream-ing from the gal- ler- y
1 x Tacet
H
Em Em7 A7 D A7
D.C. time only
(Chorus) Max - well must go free
Calls her on the phone;— "Can I— take you out— to the pic- tures,— Jo - o - o - oan?" But,
So he waits be- hind,— Writ- ing— fif - ty times—"I must not— be— so - o - o - o.— But,
Say he must go free,— The judge does— not a- gree,— and he tells— them— so - o - o - o.— But,

B
E7
A7
C
D
as she's get-ting read - y to go, A knock comes on the door.
when she turns her back on the boy, He creeps up from be-hind.
as the words are leav - ing his lips, A noise comes from be-hind.
Bang! bang! Max-well's sil - ver ham- mer came
1 X Tacet
8va bassa
(Chorus) 1 X Tacet
tu tu tu tu tu
down up-on her- head
Clang! Clang! Max - well's sil - ver ham- mer made sure that she was dead
1.
Em7

D A7 D
D
F# / C#
Bm
D7 / A
G
D
2.
Em
sure that she was dead
8va bassa
hUD
H
Cym.
T.C
Chorus D.C. time only
D
A7
oh oh oh oh
E7
tu lu tu lu lu
A7
D.C. time only
H
S

A7
Em7
A7
D
A7
D
E
to
D
F#/C#
Bm
D7/A
G
8va bassa
Coda
F#/G#
Sil - ver ham - mer man
D.C.

MEAN MR. MUSTARD

Words & Music by John Lennon & Paul McCartney.

E7
B7
D7
Sleeps in a hole in the road
Takes him out to look at the Queen
(R.H)
Sav - ing up to buy him soup clothes
on - ly place that he's e - ver been
Keeps a ten bob note up his nose,
Al - ways shouts out some-thing ob
1.
Such a

E7
C7
B7
E7
C7
B7
mean old man.
Such a mean old man.
2.
B7
B
E7
C7
B7
E7
C7
B7
scene, Such a Dirt-y old man
Dirt-y old man

MICHELLE

Words & Music by John Lennon & Paul McCartney.

B♭m7
E♭6
Ddim
C
G7-9
ma belle These are words that go to - geth - er well My Mi - chelle
Woo Woo Woo Woo Woo
C
B
F
B♭m7
E♭6
Ddim
G7-9
Mi - chelle ma belle Sont des mots qui vont tre's bien en -
Woo Woo Woo Woo Woo

C
C G7-9 C C7 Fm A♭7
- semble Tre's bien en - semble
(1x) I love you I love you I love you that's all I ___ want to
(2x) I need to I need to I need ___ to I need to ___ make you
(3x) want you I want you I want ___ you I think you ___ know by
Woo Woo Woo Woo
3x only
3x only
D♭ C7 Fm Fm FmΔ7 Fm7 Fm6
say Un - til I find a way ___ I will say the on - ly words I know That
see Oh, what you mean to me ___ Un - til I do I'm hop - ing You will
now I'll get to you some - how ___ Un - til I do I'm tell - ing you So
Woo Woo Woo Woo Woo Woo Woo Woo

to
1.
2.
D
B♭m
F
C
C
F
you'll un - der - stand
know what I
you'll un - der -
mean
I love you
Woo
(Electric Guitar)
B♭m7
E♭
Ddim
C
Bdim
C
(3x) I
Woo
Woo
Woo
Woo
Woo
Woo
D.S.

Coda
E
C
F
B♭m7
E♭6
Ddim
stand
Mi - chelle
ma belle
Sont des mots qui vont tre's bien en -
Woo
Woo
Woo
Woo
C
Bdim
C
F
Fm
FmΔ7
Fm7
Fm6
- semble
Tre's bien en - semble
And I will say the on - ly words
I know
That
Woo
Woo
Woo
(Acoustic Guitar)

Bbm/F
C
F
Bbm7
you'll un - der - stand My Mi - chelle
Woo Woo Woo
(Electric Guitar)
Eb6
Ddim
C
Bdim
C
Repeat & Fade Out

MISERY

Words & Music by John Lennon & Paul McCartney.

Intro.
F G Am G
VOCAL
The world is treat-ing me bad Mi - se - ry
OTHERS (Piano)
GUITAR I
GUITAR II
BASS
DRUMS

A
C
F
C
F
I'm the kind of guy___ who ne - ver used to cry___ The world is treat-in' me
G
C
Am
A'
C
F
bad___ mi - se - ry
I've (1.) lost her now for sure___ I
(2.3.) Send her back to me___ Cause

C
F
G
C
to
won't see her no more
It's gon - na be a drag
mi - se - ry
eve - ry - one can see
With - out her I will be
in mi - se - ry
B
Am
C
I'll re - mem - ber all the lit - tle things we've done

Am
G7
Can't she see she'll al - ways be the on - ly one on - ly one
She'll re - mem - ber and she'll miss Her lone - ly one lone - ly one
D.S.
Coda
Am
C
Am
C
Am
Oh, oh in mi - se - ry Woo my mi - se - ry La la la la la la
Fade Out

MONEY (THAT'S WHAT I WANT)

Words & Music by Berry Gordy Junior & Janie Bradford.

𝄋 (3 times Repeat)
A7
E7
B7
A
E7
A
2x, 3x
(1.) The best things in life are free
(2.) You're lov-in' giv-es me a thrill
(3. D.S.) Mo-ney don't get eve-ry-thing it's true
H
D.S.x
1x only
But you can keep them for the birds and bees Now give me mo - ney
But you're lov-in' don't pay my bills now give me mo - ney
What it don't get I can't use now give me mo - ney
That's what I
That's
What I want
(Chorus)
(Aco. piano)

E7
B7
A7
E7
want
That's what I want
yeah
That's what I want
That's
what I want
That's
what I want
That's what I want
1. 2.
B7
3.
B7
B
E7
Wah
(Aco. Piano)
(Hand Clap)

E7
B7
A7
E7
B7
Ah
Oh
D.S.
Coda
B7
C
E7
Well now give me
mo-ney
mo-ney
Ow w w
mo-ney
Wow yeah I wanna be free
Wow yeah you need mo-
That's
what I want
That's
what I want
(Chorus)
(Aco. Piano)
(Top)
(Half open)
2× B.D.

A7
E7
B7
A7
E7
B7
E7
rit.
- ney
Oh
I want mo-ney
no - - w give me mo-ney
That's
what I want
That's
what I want
That's what I want
That's what I want
That's
yeah
yeah
what I want
That's what I want
well now give me
That's what I want
That's what I want
wu

MOTHER NATURE'S SON

Words & Music by John Lennon & Paul McCartney.

1. (Straight)
2.
A
D
G/D
D
Bm
Bm7/A
Bm6/G#
Bm7/E
(1x) Born a poor young coun - try boy Mo - ther Na - tu-re's Son
(2x) Sit be - side a moun - tain stream See her wa - te-rs rise
(D.S.1x) Find me in my field of grass Mo - ther Na - tu-re's son
(D.S.2x) Ooo
(Horn)
1x, D.S.2x tacet
D.S.2x only
A
D/A
Dm7
All day long I'm sit-ting sing-ing songs for ev-ery-one
Li - st-en to the pret-ty sound of mu - sic as she flies
sway - ing dai - sies sing a la - zy song be-neath the sun
Ooo
tu tu
tu tu
to Φ
1.
D.S.1x
1x tacet
(Horn)
(Perc)
2x
1x

B
2.
D
G/D
D
D
G/D
D
DΔ7
D7
tu
tu
du tu
tu
D.S.1 x
Brass
G/D
Gm/D
D
D.S.1 X
(Dsus4)
yeah yeah yeah
D.S.1x
DS 1x
Coda
D
Dm7
G/D
D7
Ah
Mo-ther Na - tu-re's Son
D.S. 1.
2(al Coda)

MR. MOONLIGHT

Words & Music by Roy Lee Johnson.

F#
B
one sum - mer night
And from your beam you made my
dream
D#m
And from the world you sent my girl

D#m
B
F#
And from a - bove you sent us love
B
F#
D#7
G#m
And now she is mine
I think you're fine
because we love you

C#
F#
B
F#
Mis- ter Moon-light
Mis-ter Moon-light ______ , come a-gain please ______ ,
Here I am on my knees ______ beg-ging if you please

C
B
F#
D#7
And the night you don't come my way
I pray and pray more each day
because we
G#
C#
F#
to Φ
1.
D
F#
love you
Mis-ter Moon-light
H

F#
2.
F#
Coda
F#
Mis- ter Moon- light
Mis- ter Moon- light
H
D.S.
Fade Out

THE NIGHT BEFORE

Words & Music by John Lennon & Paul McCartney.

G7
A7
A
D
C
G
(AH!
The
We said our good - byes
Were you tell-ing lies?
A
night be-fore)
D
C
G
(AH!
The
A
night be-fore
(Straight)
B
Bm
Love was in your eyes
Was I so un - wise
(1x) Now to-day I
(2X, D.S.X) When I held you near
T
A
B
H
4

Gm6
Bm
Gm6
D
G7
find
You have changed your mind
You were so sin - cere
Treat me like you did the night before
Treat me like you did the night before
2x
D.S.x
3 4 5
5 6 7
D
1.
F
G
2.
D
C Am
D7
yeah
(1x) Last night is the night I will re -
(D.S.x) Last night is the night I will re -
8 9 10
10 11 12
(top center)
(shaker)

G
C
G
G
Bm
E7
A7
- mem - ber you by
When I think of things we did It makes me wan-na cry
- mem - ber you by
When I think of things we did It makes me wan-na cry
D.S.x(
D.S.x
(TOP SIDE)
D
C
G(AH!
The night be-fore
A
D
We said our good - byes
Love was in your
Were you tell-ing lies
Was I so un -
(TOP SIDE)

C
G (AH!
A
The night be-fore
E Bm
Gm6
Bm
eyes
wise
Now to-day I find
When I held your near
You have changed your mind
You were so sin-
cere
Gm6
D
G7
to
D
F
G
F D
Treat me like you did the night before
Treat me like you did the night before
Yes
C UD
D.S.x

C
G
A
D
C
G
A
Coda
D
F
D7
D
Like the night be - fore
D.S.

NO REPLY

Words & Music by John Lennon & Paul McCartney.

Em
F∆7
Em
C
Dm7
I saw the light
I near-ly died
I know that you saw me
'cause you walked hand in hand
'cause I looked up to
with an-oth-er
G
C
to
1.
2.
D
C
see your face
man in my place
I tried to te-le-
If I were you I'd
(Hand Clap)
E
A
Dm
F
re-al-ise that I
love you more than a-ny o-ther

C
C
E
A
guy
And I'll for - give
the
lie
that
I
Dm
F
C
heard be - fore
when you gave
me
no
re - ply
I tried to te - le -
D.S.
Coda
C
Am
Em
FΔ7
C69
No re - ply
no re - ply

NORWEGIAN WOOD

Words & Music by John Lennon & Paul McCartney.

E
A
E
I once_ had a girl_ Or should I say she once had me. She showed_ me her room is-n't it
good Nor-we-gian wood? She
B
Em
asked me to stay And she told me To sit a-ny-where___
told me she worked in the morn-ing And start-ed to laugh___
A
So
I
1xonly
2xonly play (Tambourine)
(Bass Drum)
(1x Bass Drum)

Em
F#m7
B7
C
E
I looked a-round And I no-ticed there was-n't a chair
told her I did-n't And crawled off to sleep in the bath
I sat on a rug bi-ding my
And when I a-woke I was a-
T
A
B
E
1.
time Drink-ing her wine
-lone This bird had flown
We talked un-til two And then she said "it's time for bed"
So I lit a fire Is-n't it
2xonly play

D
E
She
2.
E
good Nor-we-gian wood ?
E

NOT A SECOND TIME

Words & Music by John Lennon & Paul McCartney.

1.
2.
G
D.C.1x
D7
Am7
D7
B Am7
you
D.C.1x (yeah)
through
oh.
(1x, D.C.) You're giv-ing me the
Bm7
G
Em
Am
same old line
I'm wond'-ring why.
You hurt me then
You're back a-gain
D.C.x
H

Bm
D7
Em
C
to
Am7
No no no, not a sec-ond time
D.C.x
Not a sec-ond
(Solo)
Bm7
G
Em
Am
(No Crash)

Coda
D
Bm
D7
Em
G
time
Em
G
Em
G
(Chorus) not the sec-ond time
not the sec-ond time
no no no no no
no no no
D.C.
Fade Out

NOWHERE MAN

Words & Music by John Lennon & Paul McCartney.

Am
to Φ
E
B
E
B
no - where plans For no - bo - dy
(1.3.) Does-n't have a point of view
(2.) He's as blind as he can be
1x only
A
E
F#m
Am
E
knows not where he's go - ing to
Just sees what he wants to see
Is - n't he a bit like you and me?
No-where man Can you see me at all?

C
E
G#m
A
G#m
A
No-where man please li-sten You don't know what you're miss-ing No-where man
No-where man don't wo-rry Take your time, don't hur-ry Leave it all
Ah Ah la la la Ah Ah la la la
G#m
F#m7
1.
B7
D
E
The world is at your com-mand
till some-bo-dy else Lends you a hand
Ah Ah la la la Ah Ah la la la la
1 X Tacet

B
A
E
F#m
Am
E
2.
B7
3.
B7
Ah
1a 1a 1a 1a
Ah
1a 1a 1a 1a
Harm.
Harm
S P
D.C.

Coda
E
F#m
Am
E
no - bo-dy
Ma-king all his no-where plans for no - bo-dy
no - bo-dy
Ma-king all his no-where plans for no - bo-dy
F#m
Am
E
Ma-king all his no-where plans for no-bo-dy
Ma-king all his no-where plans for no-bo-dy

OB-LA-DI OB-LA-DA

Words & Music by John Lennon & Paul McCartney.

1. (Straight)
2.
A
B♭
F7
E♭
(1x) Des-mond has a bar-row in the mar-ket place Mol - ly is the sin-ger in a band Des - mond says to Mol-ly girl I like your face And Mol-ly
(2x) Des-mond takes a trol-ley to the jewel-lers store Buys a twen-ty ca-rat gol-den ring rin-ring Takes it back to Mol-ly wait-ing at the door And as he
(DS.1X, DS.2x) Hap-py ev-er af-ter in the mar-ket place Des - mond lets the child-ren lend a hand Mol - ly stays at home and does her pre-tty face And in the
D.S.2x (his)
D.S.2x
D.S.1x D.S.2x
8va
Perc.

2x Chorus
B♭
F7
B♭
Ob - la - di
B
La La La La La La La La
says this as she takes him by the hand
gives it to her she be - gins to sing sin - sing
eve - ning she's a sin - ger with the band Yeah
Ob - la - di ob - la - da life goes on
D.S.1x D.S.2x Brass.
D.S. 2x
Dm7
F
Gm7
La La La La La
La La how the life goes on
La la la la la la la la
bra La la how the life goes on
Ob - la - di ob - la - da life goes on

Dm7
F
Gm7
B♭
F7
1a 1a 1a 1a
La 1a how the life goes on
1.
B♭
2. B♭
B♭7
bra
La 1a how the life goes on
Yeah
D.S.1X
gliss
D.S.1X
C
E♭
B♭
(A♭)
B♭
In a couple of years they have built a home sweet home
D.S.1x Shaker

E♭
B♭/F
F7
ha ha ha ha
With a couple of kids run-ning in the yard of Des-mond and Mol - ly Jones
D.S. 1x
shaker
wood Block
D.S. 1. D.S. 2(al Coda)
Coda
Gm
F7
B♭
ha ha ha ha ha ha ha ha ha ha ha ha ha ha ha ha ha ha ha ha ha ha ha ha ha ha Thank you Ooo ha ha ha
And if you want some fun take Ob - la - di ob - la - da (Free)
Flore Tom

OCTOPUS'S GARDEN

Words & Music by Ringo Starr.

A
E
C#m
A
B
I'd like to be under the sea In an oc - to - pu-s's gar - den in the shade
We would be warm be - low the storm In our lit-tle hide a-way be-neath the waves
We would shout and swim a-bout the co - ral that lies be-neath the waves
(Chorus)
1 x Tacet
Ooo
Ooo
Ah Ah Ah
(Piano)
2 x only
He'd let us in knows where we've been In his oc - to - pu-s's gar - den in the shade
Rest - ing our head on the sea bed In an oc - to - pu-s's gar - den near a cave.
Oh what joy for eve - ry girl and boy Know - ing they're hap - py and their safe
Ah
Ooo
Ooo
(2x) Ah Ah Ah
(3x) Hap - py and their
2 x only
B.G. simile
8va
1 x only

B
C#m
C#m
C#m/B
A
B
I'd ask my friends to come and see In an oc-to-pu-s's gar-den with me
We would sing and dance a-rou-nd be-cause we know we can't be found
We would be so hap-py you and me No one there to tell us what to do
Ah
safe
2x
T
A
B
4 5 6
4 5 6
5 6 7
7 8 9
Cym.
C
E
C#m
A
B
1.
E
I'd like to be un-der the sea, In an oc-to-pu-s's gar-den in the shade
D.S. time only
Ah
Ah
B.G. Simile
(B.G.)
8va
1 2 3
4 5 6
5 6 7
7 8 9
1 2 3
H.H.

2.
D
E
A
(S.E. Voice)
F#m
D
Ah
Ah
Ah
Ah
Ah
8va
(E. Guitar)
E
A
F#m
D
E
Ah
Ah
Ah
Ah
Ah

A
B7
Ah
D.S.
Coda
A
B
C#m
B
oc - to - pu-s's gar - den with__you in an
Ah
Ooo
Ah
B.G. simile
A
B
C#m
B
A
B
A
oc - to - pu-s's gar - den with__you in an oc - to - pu-s's gar - den with you
Ah
Ooo
Ah
Ah
8va

OH! DARLING

Words & Music by John Lennon & Paul McCartney.

D
Bm
E
Bm
E
harm.
Be-lieve
me when I tell you,
I'll
ne - ver do
you,
no
Ah
Ah
Ah
10 11 12
7 8 9
12 13 14
A
D
A
E7
B
A
harm.
Oh!
Oh!
Oh!
Dar - ling,
Dar - ling,
Dar - ling,
if you
if you
please be -
2 x Tacet
Ooo
9 10 11
10 11 12
9 10 11
9 10 11

E
F#m
D
leave me, I'll nev - er make it a-lone. Be-lieve
leave me, I'll nev - er make it a-lone. Be-lieve
lieve me, I'll nev - er let you down. Oh, be-lieve me dar-ling Be-lieve
3X
ooo
ooo
Ah
12 13 14
5 6 7
10 11 12
Bm
E
Bm
E
to Φ
A
B
me when I tell you, ooo Don't ev - er leave me a-lone.
me when I tell you, I'll nev - er do you no harm.
me when I tell you, ooo I'll nev - er do you no
Ah
Ah
7 8 9
12 13 14
9 10 11
10 11 12

C
A
A7
D
F
2x (Be-lieve me dar-ling)
When you told me
You did-n't need me a-ny-more,
Well, you
simile
A
A7
B
know I near-ly broke_down and cried.
When you told me
you did-n't need me a-ny-more,
Well, you

E
F
1.
E
Eaug7
2.
E
Eaug7
know I near - ly broke down and died.
Oh!
died.
Oh!
8va
D.S.
Coda
A
D
A
B♭7
A
Tempo Rubato
harm.
(Synth.)
8va bassa
T.C

OLD BROWN SHOE

Words & Music by George Harrison.

C7
Dm7
___ is on - ly half of wha - t's wrong ___
___ some try to drag me ___ do - wn ___
___ that love is some-thing I'd ha - te ___
I want a Short-haired girl ___ who
And when I see your smile ___ re -
I'll make an ear - ly start ___ I'm
some-times wears it twice as long ___
- plac - ing ev - 'ry thought - less frown ___
mak - ing sure that I'm not late ___
F
Now I'm step-pin'out this old ___
So es - cap - ing from this zoo ___
For your sweet top lip I'm in
D.S. 2x
D.S. 2x
2x D.S. 2x

F7
A♭
A♭7
F
brown shoe
Ba - by I'm in love with you
I'm so glad you came here it won't
Ba - by I'm in love with you
I'm so glad you came here it won't
the queue
Ba - by I'm in love with you
I'm so glad you came here it won't
Eaug
Am
to ⊕
C7
be the same now I'm tell-ing you
be the same now when I'm with you
be the same now when I'm with you
I'm
2x. D.S. 2x
D.S. 2x

1.
B
2.
C7
G
F
Though you (1x) If I grow up I'll be a sing - er wear-ing rings on ev - 'ry fin-ger
(D.S.1x) I may ap-pear to be im-per - fect my love is some-thing you can't re-ject
D.S.2x
S
T
A
B
G
F
F#dim
Not wor-ry-ing what they or you'll say I'll live and love and may-be some - day who knows ba - by
I'm chang-ing fast-er than the wea - ther If you and me should get to - ge - ther who knows ba - by

F#dim
G
to Φ 1.
G7
C
C7
You may com - fort me
You may com - fort me
Heh!
Dm7

Dm7
F
F7
A♭
A♭7
F
Eaug
Am
Am
D.S. 1

Coda 1.
G7
Heh!
I know my
D.S. 2.
Coda 2.
F
Eaug
so glad you came here it won't be the same now when
Am
I'm with you
Yeah yeah yeah
D (1x 2x 3x 4x tacet)
Tu la
Tu ru tu
1,2,3,4x tacet
(1x only crash.)
Repeat & Fade Out

ONE AFTER 909

Words & Music by John Lennon & Paul McCartney.

B7
A
B7
My ba - by says she's trav-'ling on the One Af - ter Nine - O - Nine
begged her not to go and I begged her on my bend - ed knees
I said move o - ver hon - ey. I'm trav-el-ing on that line
You-'re on - ly fooling a-round. You're on - ly fool-ing a-round with me
I said

B7
E7
B7
move over once
move over twice
come on ba - by, don't be cold as ice
(I) said I'm trav - 'ling on the
gliss.
F#7
1.
B7
2.
B7
One Af - ter Nine - O - Nine
I

B
E7
B7
C#7
I've got my bag,
D.S.time only
run to the sta - tion
Rail - man says
D.S.time
F#7
E7
you've got the wrong lo - cation
D.S.time only (Yeah)
picked up my bags
8va

B7
C#7
run right home
D.S. time only
(run right home)
Then I find
I've got the
h.C
h.U
F#7
num-ber wrong
well
C
(I) said I'm trav'ling on the One Af - ter Nine - O-Nine
8va
P

B7
I said, move o - ver hon-ey. I'm trav-el-ing on __ that line __
I said
C
P
T
A
B
B7
move over once __
move over twice __
gliss.
E7
come on ba - by don't be __ cold as ice __
to

B7
F#7
B7
D
B7
(I) said I'm trav-'ling on the One Af - ter Nine - O-Nine
Yeah
Port. C
h.C
8va

B7
E7
B7
F#7
B7
D.S.

Coda
B7
F#7
B7
F#7
(I) said we're trav-'ling on the One Af - ter Nine - O,
I said we're trav-'ling on the One Af - ter Nine - O,
B7
F#7
B7
(I) said we're trav-'ling on the One Af - ter Nine - O - Nine

ONLY A NORTHERN SONG

Words & Music by George Harrison.

A
Bm7
(A) D.S.x
this song
at night
mo - ny
You may think the chords are go - ing wrong
You may think the bands are not quite right
Is a lit - tle dark and out of key
But they're not
But they are
You're cor-rect
2x
E7
D
1.
He just wrote it like that
They just play it like that
There's no - bo - dy there

B
D
E
Bm7
G
C#7
F#7
Bm
D.S.time
it (1x) does-n't real-ly mat-ter what chords I play what words I say or time of day it
(2x) does-n't real-ly mat-ter what clothes I wear or how I fare or if my hair is
(D.S.x) (Instrumental)
2x →
T
A
B
F#7
D
A
(C#) 2x D.S.x
E
B
1.
C
A
is As it's on ly a North-ern Song
brown When it's on ly a North-ern Song
And I told you there no one there
(Acoustic Piano)
2x D.S.x

A
Bm7
E7
D
T
A
B

to ⊕
2.
⊕ Coda D
D
E
E
Bm7
G
C#7
D.S.time
It
D.S.
F#7
Bm
F#7
D
A
C#

E/B
E A
Bm7
T
A
B
Fade Out

PAPERBACK WRITER

Words & Music by John Lennon & Paul McCartney.

G7
A
G7
Dear Sir or Ma-dam will you read my book? It took me years to write,___ will you
thou - sand pa-ges, give or take a few; I'll be writ - ing more___ in a
1x Tacet
Ah
Ah
Ah
take a look? Based on a nov-el by a man named Lear and I need a job___ so I want to be a pa-per-back
week or two. I can make it long-er if you like the style, I can change it 'round___ and I want to be a pa-per-back
Ah
Ah
Ah
Ah
Ah

C
G7
B
G7
writ - er paper-back writ - er. It's the dirt - y sto - ry of a
writ - er pa - per-back writ - er. If you real - ly like it you can
pa - per back writ - er.
Ah
1 x Tacet
dirt - y man, and his cling - ing wife doesn't un-der-stand. His son is work - ing for the Dail - y Mail; It's a
have the rights, It could make a mil - lion for you ov - er night. If you must re-turn it you can send it here, But I
Ah
Ah
Ah
Ah
Ah
H
1 2 3

G7
C
G7
steady - y job But he wants to be a pa-per-back writ - er pa - per-back writ - er.
need a break and I want to be a pa-per-back writ - er pa - per-back writ - er.
Ah
Ah
pa - per-back writ - er.
C
N.C.
writ - er writ - er
pa - per-back writ - er
pa - per-back
writ - er, writ - er

G7
1.
2.
G7
It's a
D
G
pa - per - back writ - er
Pa - per - back writ - er
Repeat & Fade Out

PENNY LANE

Words & Music by John Lennon & Paul McCartney.

Bm7
Bm6
G#
GΔ7
F#7sus4
F#7
F#7sus4
F#7
And all the peo-ple that come and go
stop and say hel-lo
On the
B
B
C#m7
F#7
B
Bm7
(1X) cor-ner is a bank-er with a mo-tor car
the lit-tle child-ren laugh at him be-hind his back
And the
(D.S.X) the bar-ber shaves an-oth-er cus-tom-er
we see the bank-er sit-ting wait-ing for a trick
And then the
(D.S.x tacet)
8va
1x tacet
T
A
B

Bm6/G#
GΔ7
F#7sus4
F#7
E
C
A
bank-er ne-ver wears a "mac" in the pour - ing rain ve-ry strange Pen-ny Lane (1X D.S.x) is in my ears
fi-re man rush-es in from the pour - ing rain ve-ry strange Pen-ny Lane (2X) is in my ears
D.S.x
(H.H)
A/C#
D
D 1x(A)
A
A/C#
and in my eyes Wet be-neath the blue sub-ur-ban skies
and in my eyes Full of fish and fin - ger pies

D
to Φ
F#7
D
B
C#m7
F#7
I sit and mean while back in Pen-ny Lane there is a fire-man with an ho-ur glass And in his pock-
in sum-mer mean while back be-hind the shel-ter in the mid-dle of the round a-bout A pret-ty nurse
(2x tacet)
(1x tacet)
B
Bm7
Bm6
G#
GΔ7
F#7sus4
F#7
-et is a port-rait of the Queen He likes to keep his fi-re en-gine clean It's a clean ma-chine
-is sell-ing pop-pies from a tray And tho' she feels as if she's in a play She is an-y way
2x

1.
E
F#7 sus4
F#7
B
C#m7
F#7
B
Bm7
Ah
Ah
Ah
(Piccolo Trumpet)
(Top)
Bell
Bm7/G#
GΔ7
F#7 sus4
F#7
E
2.
F#7 sus4
F#7
Ah
Pen-ny Lane
Pen-ny Lane
D.S.

Coda
F♯7
F
B
B/D♯
E
mean-while back Pen-ny Lane
is in my ears
and in my eyes
8va
B
B/D♯
E
E/B
B
There be-neath the blue
surb-ur-ban skies
Pen-ny Lane
8 beat
gliss.
gliss.

PIGGIES

Words & Music by George Harrison.

A♭ E♭ Fm B♭7 Fm B♭7 E♭ to ⊕
And for all__ the lit-tle pig-gies Life is get-ting worse__ Al-ways hav-ing dirt__ to play a-round in
You will find__ the big-ger pig-gies Stir-ring up the dirt__ Al-ways have clean shirts to play a-round in
You can see them out for din-ner With their pig-gy wives__ Clutch-ing forks and knives to eat their ba-con
D.S.X
G D Em A7 Em A7 D
2x
1 2 3
1. A♭ E♭ A♭ E♭
2. A♭ E♭ A♭ C7
B B♭m C7
In their sties with all their back-ing
G D G D G D G B7 Am B7
1 2 3

D♭
A♭/E♭
E♭
B♭m
C7
D♭
E♭
They don't care what goes on__ a-round
In their eyes__ there's some-thing lack-ing What they need's a darn good whacking
C
G
D
Am
B7
C
D
1 2 3
C
A♭
E♭
A♭
E♭
A♭
E♭
Fm
B♭7
D
G
D
G
D
G
D
Em
A7
1 2 3

Fm B♭7 E♭ A♭ E♭ A♭ E♭
Coda
A♭ E♭
Em A7 D G D G D
G D
D.S.
A♭m E♭ A♭m E♭ B♭7 E♭
A (Slow) E
one more time
Gm D Gm D A7 D

PLEASE MR. POSTMAN

Words & Music by B. Holland & F.C. Gorman.

A
F#m
D
E
Oh___ yeah___
Oh___ yeah___
Please__ Please___ Mis-ter Po - st-man__ oh___ Yeah___
Please__ Please___ Mis-ter Po - st-man__ oh___ Yeah___
look and see___ Is there's a let-ter in the bag for me___ I've been wait-ing___a long long time___ Since I heard from that
H.H open
C
2x
There must__ be some mail to-day___ From my girl friend so far a-way__
so ma-ny days__ you past me by___ See the tears stand-ing in my eye__
gal of mine___ Wu___ Wu___

D
1.
D
2x
E
A
Please Mis-ter Post-man look and see If there's a let-ter a let-ter for me I've be-en stan-ding he-re
You did-n't stop to make me fe-el bet-ter By leav-ing me a card or a let-ter Mis-ter
Wu
F#m
wai-ting Mis-ter Post - man So pa-tien-tly for just a card or just a let-ter

E
2.
E
A
F#m
Say-ing she's re-turn-ing home to me Please Mis-ter Post-man look and see Is there a let-ter,
(chorus C 1~8)
Wu
Mis-ter Post-man look and see Is there a let-ter in the
1 2 3
1 2 3
2 3 4
D
E
yeah, for me I've be-en wait-ing such a long time Since I heard from that gal of mine You got-ta
bag for me I've been wait-ing a long long time Since I heard from that gal of mine
1 2 3
1 2 3

F
A
(3times)
F#m
2x
D
(1.3.) Wait a min-ute wait a min-ute Oh yeah wait a min-ute wait a min-ute Oh yeah you got-ta wait a min-ute wait a min-ute
(2) Wait a min-ute wait a min-ute Oh yeah wait a min-ute wait a min-ute Oh yeah Mis-ter Post - - - man
3x
Wait a min-ute wait a min-ute Mis-ter Post - man wait a min-ute wait a min-ute Mis-ter Post - man wait a min-ute wait a min-ute
T
A
B
1 2 3
2 3 4
1 2 3
1. 2.
E
3.
E
Oh yeah (you got-ta) check it and see one more time for me you got-ta wait a min-ute wait a min-ute oh yeah you got-ta
Oh yeah de - li-ver the let - ter The soon - er the better you got-ta
Mis-ter Post - man wait a min-ute wait a min-ute Mis-ter Post - man
Fade Out

PLEASE PLEASE ME

Words & Music by John Lennon & Paul McCartney.

E
A
E
G
A
B
E
said these words to my girl,
me to show the way, love,
I know you nev - er e - ven
Why do I al - ways have to
(Tom)
A
E
C
A
F#m
C#m
A
Come on,
Come on,
Come on,
Come on,
Please,
try, girl.
say, love.
Come on, Come on, Come on, Come on, Please,

E A B to Φ
Please me, wo yeah, like I please
1. E A B
you.
2. E
you.
Please me, wo__ yeah, like I please you.
you.
T A B
1 2 3
2 3 4
S
(T.T.)
D A B E A
Ah ah ah In__ my heart Ah
I don't want to sound com-plain-ing, but you know there's al-ways rain in my____ heart.
I do all the pleas-ing with you,

B
ah
E
with you,
wo
A
yeah,
B
why do you make me blue?
E
A
B
it's so hard to rea-son with you, wo— yeah, why do you make me blue?
D.S.
Coda
E
you
wo—
A
yeah,
B
like I please
E
you,
wo—
A
yeah,
B
like I please
E
you
G
C
B
E
you, wo— yeah, like I please you, wo— yeah, like I please, you.

POLYTHENE PAM

Words & Music by John Lennon & Paul McCartney.

A
D
A
E
see Pol - y - thene Pam
dose of her in jack-boot and kilt,
She's so good - look - ing But she looks like a man.
She's kil - ler dil - ler when she's dressed to the hilt.
Well, you should
She's the
Ah
G
B7
C
E
see her in drag, dressed in her pol - y - thene bag, Yes, you should see Pol - y - thene Pam.
kind of a girl that makes the news of the world Yes, you could say she was at - tract - ive - ly built.
S

C D E D A E D A
Yeh, yeh, yeh.
Yeh, yeh, yeh.
1. 2.
E E B D A E D A E
Get a
C D H P
H

E
D A E
D A E
C
UD P
UD P
C
UD P
UD P
D A E
D A E
D A E
1hC
P
C
C D
C
C
P
1hC
P
C
C D
C
C
P

E
D
A
E
E
C
E
D
C#m
E7/B
vib

P.S. I LOVE YOU

Words & Music by John Lennon & Paul McCartney.

D A Bm A B♭
- ther Keep all my love for - e - ver P. S. I love you
love Un - til the day I do love P. S. I love you
C D
you you you
you you you
C
G D
As I write this let - ter 2x (oh)
G D G D D A
Send my love to you (you know I want you to) Re - mem - ber that I'll al - ways (yeah) Be in love with
T
A
B

Coda
to Coda
D
Em
A
Bm
B♭
C
you
I'll be com - ing home a-gain to you love Un - til the day I
do love P. S. I love you
you you you
I love you

RAIN

Words & Music by John Lennon & Paul McCartney.

A
G
C
G
C
G
rain comes they run and hide their heads, they might as well be dead. If the
sun shines they slip in - to the shade and sip their lem - on - ade. When the
1 x Tacet
When the sun - shines, ah
When the sun shines,
H
P
S
C
1.
2.
rain comes, if the rain comes. When the sun
sun shines, When the
ah
sun

B
shines.
Rain
shines.
Rain
8va
2×
(Tambourine)
G
I don't mind.
Shine
I don't mind.
Shine

C
G
G
C
G
the weath-er's fine.
I can show you that
Can you hear me? that
the weath-er's fine.
C
G
G
C
when it starts to rain ev-'ry-thing's the same. I can show you.
when it rains and shines it's just a state of mind. Can you hear me?
when the rain comes, ah when the rain comes, ah
when it rains and shines when it rains and shines

to Φ
Φ Coda
C
G
G
I can show you.
Can you hear
me?
I can show you
Can you hear
me?
H
S
D.S.
D
G
E
G
8va bassa

G
(Ad-lib.～)
Ah
8va bassa
H
Ah
8va. bassa
8va. bassa.
Fade Out

REVOLUTION

Words & Music by John Lennon & Paul McCartney.

A
B♭
E♭
(1x) say you want a re - vo - lu - tion Well you know
(2x) say you got a real so - lu - tion Well you know
(D.S.x) say you'll change the con-sti - tu - tion Well you know
We all want to change the world
We'd all love to see the plan
We all want to change your head
D.S.x
W.C
2x, D.S.x
B
You tell me that it's e-vo - lu - tion Well you know
You ask me for a con-tri - bu - tion Well you know
You tell me it's the in-sti - tu - tion Well you know

E♭
F7
We all want to change the world
We're do - ing what we can
You better free your mind in - stead
C
Cm/G
F7
Cm/G
A♭ B♭ G
But when you talk a - bout de - struc-tion
But when you want mo-ney for peo-ple with minds that hate
But if you go car-ry-ing pic-tures of Chair-man Mao
Don't you know that you can count me out
All I can tell you is bro-ther you have to wait
You ain't going to make it with a - ny - one a - ny - how
D.S.x

D
G
F7
B♭
E♭
Don't you know it's gon-na be
al - right
8va.
to Φ
1.
2x, D.S.x

F7
2.
F7
E
B♭
You
Ah
Ah ah ah ah
H
E♭
ah ah ah ah
ah ah
ah ah ah ah
ah ah ah ah
F7
ah ah ah ah
W.C

F7
You
8va
D.S.
Coda
F7
F
B♭
al - right
al - right
tr.
W.C
U
gliss.

E♭
B♭
E♭
B♭
al - right
al - right
al - right
al - right
E♭
F
B♭
C♭6
B♭6
al - right
al - right

REVOLUTION 1

Words & Music by John Lennon & Paul McCartney.

E
A
upper part 1x tacet
You say you want a re - vo - lu - tion, Well you know
say you got a real so - lu - tion, Well you know
say you'll change the con - sti - tu - tion, Well you know
(Brass 1x tacet, 2x low part only play)
h.c D
8va. bassa
1 x only
E.Gt.
D
We all want to change the world.
We'd all love to see the plan.
We all want to change your head.
You
You
You
3x chorus
Ah.
Shoo - bee-doo - wap
3x only

A
D
tell me that it's e - vo - lu - tion, Well you know,
ask me for a con - tri - bu - tion, Well you know,
tell me it's the in - sti - tu - tion, Well you know,
We all want to change the
We're do - ing want we
You better free your mind in -
(2x, 3x chorus)
Ah,
3x only
3x only
D
E
world.
can.
- stead.
Shoo - bee - doo - wap
Ah,
Shoo - bee - doo - wap
L1x Tacet
L1x tacet
B
Bm
E
But when you talk a - bout de struc - tion,
But when you want mon - ey for peo - ple with minds that hate,
But if you go car - ry - ing pic - tures of chair - man Mao,

Bm
G A F#
E
Don't you know that you can count me out.
All I can tell you is bro-ther you have to wait.
You ain't going to make it with an-y-one an-y-how.
Don't you know it's gon-na be
Ah,
1x tacet
C
A
D (D/A)
A
D
al - right, Don't you know it's gon-na be al - right, Don't you know it's gon-na be
shoo - bee-doo - wap Ah, shoo - bee-doo - wap Ah, shoo - bee-doo - wap Ah, shoo - bee-doo - wap Ah,

A
D
al - right
shoo - bee-doo - wap
Ah,
shoo - bee-doo - wap
1. 2.
E
Ah
3
E
Ah
D
A
8va. bassa
Ah, shoo - bee-doo - wap Ah, shoo - bee-doo - wap Ah,
Ah Ah Ah Ah

A
D
A
Ah Ah Ah Ah Ah Ah Al. - right al - right al - right al - right al - right
shoo - bee-doo - wap Ah, shoo - bee-doo - wap Ah, shoo - bee-doo - wap Ah, shoo - bee-doo - wap Ah, shoo - bee-doo - wap Ah,
al - right al - right al right al - right
Ah Ah Ah
shoo - bee-doo - wap Ah, shoo - bee-doo - wap Ah, shoo - bee-doo - wap Ah, shoo - bee-doo - wap Ah,

D/A
A
D/A
A
Ah Ah Ah Ah Ah
shoo - bee-doo - wap Ah, shoo - bee-doo - wap Ah, shoo - bee-doo - wap Ah, shoo - bee-doo - wap Ah,
al - right al - right
shoo - bee-doo - wap Ah, shoo - bee-doo - wap Ah, shoo - bee-doo - wap Ah, shoo - bee-doo - wap Ah,
Fade Out

REVOLUTION 9

Words & Music by John Lennon & Paul McCartney.

Bm
C#sus4
Bm
-ber 9 Num-ber 9 Num-ber 9 Num-ber 9 Num-ber 9 Num-ber 9 Num-
(Clarinet)
poco rit.
(Strings)
(Acoustic Bass)
C Fm
E♭
D D♭m (Tempo up) (x4)
D♭m D♭m7
-ber 9 Num-ber 9 Num-ber 9 Num-ber 9 Num-ber 9 Num-
(1x only)
(Tape Reverse)
(1x only)
(Tape Reverse)
(Electric Bass)
(1x 2x 3x Tacet)
(1x only)
(1x 2x 3x Tacet)
(Tape Reverse)
(Noise)

E
N.C.
(Tempo down)
(x3)
1. 2.
F
3. B♭ (Tempo down)
(Chorus 1x2xTacet)
(Orchestra)
(Brass)
(Crash)
(Crash 1x2xTacet)
(Timpani roll)
G
N.C.
(Talking)
(Tape Reverse)
(Strings Tape Reverse)
(Tape Reverse)
(Crash)
(Noise)
H
D♭m
(Tempo up)
D♭m
D♭m7

I
Bm
(Tempo down)
Em
Bm
F#
(Clarinet)
rit.
(Acoustic Bass)
T
A
B
J
Fm
(Tempo down)
Eb
K
N.C.
(x3)
1. 2.
(2x 3x Laughing)
(Tape Reverse) (3x Tape Cut)
(1x only)
(Orchestra)(1xTacet)
(1x only)
(Brass) (1x Tacet)
(Reverse Guitar)
(1x Tacet)
(Crash)
(Timpani roll)

L
3.
(Tempo down)
Num-ber 9 Num-ber 9
M
(Tempo up)
Num-ber 9 Num - ber 9 Num-ber 9 Num-ber 9
(Talking & Baby's Laughing)
(Talking)
(Piano)
N
Bm
Em
Bm
Em
Num-ber 9 Num-ber 9 Num-ber 9
(Brass)

O
F
(Tempo down)
B♭
N.C.
(Crowded & Number 9)
P
F -9
Number 9
B♭
2x
(Crowded & Voices)
1. N.C.
(Chorus)
(2x only)
2x
(Tape Reverse)
5 5 5 5 5 5 5 5 5 5 5 5
2x
Bell
Noise
Q
2. C
F
C
(Tempo up)
(x3)
C
G
3x
R
N.C.
(Crowded & Talking)
(Clarinet)
(Oboe)
(Orchestra)
2x
(Brass)
(Noise & Klaxon)
(Noise)

S
Bm
(Tempo down)
(Talking)
F#(onC#)
Bm
N.C.
(Crowded & Voices)
(Tape Reverse)
T
(Tempo up)
(×7)
(Crowded & Talking & Voices)
7X
U
Bm
(Tempo down)
N.C.
(Cello)
(Tape Reverse)
(Tape Reverse)

V
(x6)
(Crowded & Voiced & Number 9)
(Talking & Voices)
W (Tempo up)
(x7)
(Talking & Demonstration)
(Tape Reverse)
(Clarinet) (1x, 2x, 3x Tacet)
(Tape Reverse)
(Electric Piano)
(Guitar)
(Strings)
(Brass)
(Tape Reverse)
(Bass) (1x, 2x Tacet)
(Crash)
(Timpani roll & Noise)
(Claps)
(Noise)
X F
B♭
N.C.
(Tempo down)
(Talking)
(Voices)
(Chorus)
(Piano)
(Orchestra)
(Rain)
(War)

Y
(Tempo up)
(Crowded & Talking)
Z
(Tempo down)
(Crowded & Talking)
(Clarinet)
(Strings)
(2x)
(Orchestra)
(Tape Reverse)
T
A
B
(2x)
(Noise)
A'
Bm
(Tempo up)
F#
Bm
N.C.
(Tempo up)
(Crowded & Talking & Number 9)
(Crowded & Talking)
(Clarinet)
rit.
a tempo
(Brass)
T
A
B
(Crash)
(March)

B'
Am
C' N.C.
(Talking)
(Crowded & Talking)
(Girl's talking & Voices)
(Chorus)
gliss.
Snare roll
(Noise)
D' E (Tempo down) (×3)
E' N.C. (Tempo down)
(Demonstration with Panning)
(Opera)
(3× rit.)
Repeat & Fade Out

ROCK AND ROLL MUSIC

Words & Music by Chuck Berry.

A7
D7
A7
it, It's got a back beat you can't lose it, A - ny old time you use it. It's

E7
A7
E7
A7
got-ta be Rock Roll Mu - sic, If you wan-na dance with me If you wan-na dance with me
5x only
gliss.

1. 2. 3. 4.
A7
B E7
A7
I've got no kick a-gain-st mod - ern jazz, Un-less they try to play it too darn fast; And change the beau-ty of the
I took my loved one o-ver 'cross the tracks, So she can hear my man a - wail a sax; I must ad-mit they have a
'Way down South they gave a ju - bi-lee, The joke-y folks they had a jam-bo - ree; They're drink-in' home-brew from a
Don't care to hear 'em play a tan - go, I'm in the mood to hear a mam - bo; It's way to ear-ly for a
gliss.
T
A
B
D7
E7
5.
A7
me-lo - dy, Un-til they sound just like a sym-pho-ny That's why I go for that
rock-in' band, Man, they were go-in' like a hur-ri-can' That's why I go for that
wa-ter cup, The folks danc-in' got all shook up And start-ed play-in' that
con - go, So keep a-rock-in' that pi - a - no So I can hear some of that

ROCKY RACCOON

Words & Music by John Lennon & Paul McCartney.

G7
G
C
C/B
Am7
And one day his wo-man ran off with a-no-ther guy
Hit young Roc-ky in the eye
Roc-ky did-n't like that he said I'm
Dsus4
D
G7
C
C/B
gon-na get that boy
so one day he walked in-to town Booked him-self a room in the lo-cal sal-oon
(Harmonica)

B
Am7
Dsus4
D
G7
C
C/B
Roc-ky Ra-ccoon checked in-to his room On-ly to find Gide-on's bib-le Roc-
-ky had come e-quipped with the gun to shoot off the legs of his ri-val His
2x
(Brush) 1x Tacet
1x in
C
Am7
Dsus4
D
G7
C
C/B
ri-val it seems had bro-ken his dreams By steal-ing the girl of his fan-cy her
name was Mag-ill and she called her-self Lil But eve-ry-one knew her as Nan-cy Now
1x with tremolo
2x
2x
2x
snare

D
(Straight)
Am7
Dsus4
D
G7
C
C/B
she and her man
who called him-self Dan
Were in the next room at the hoe-down
Roc-ky burst in
and grin-ning a grin
He said Dan-ny boy this is a show-down
Roc-ky Rac-coon
he fell back in his room
on-ly to find Gid-eon's bi-ble
(Chorus) D.S. x
2x
da
D.S.x
D.S.x (D.S.x with tremolo)
E
Am7
Dsus4
D
G7
C
C/B
Dani-el was hot
he drew first and shot
And Roc-ky colla-psed in the cor-ner
Gide-on checked out
And he left it no doubt
To help with good Roc-ky's re-vi-val
Ah
Oh Yeah Yeah
oh
D.S. (D.S.x with tremolo)

F (D.S.x with Repeat)
Am7
Dsus4
D
G7
to Φ
(Repeat)
1.
C
C/B
(1x) da
da
2x D.S.1x D.S.2x da
(D.S.2x) Come on Roc-ky boy
Come on Roc-ky boy
(Honky Tonk Piano)
tr.
D.S.2x
2.
C
C/B
G
Am7
Dsus4
D
G7
da
da
Now the doc-tor came in
stink-ing of gin
And pro-cee-ded to lie on the ta-
(Accoudion)

C
C/B
Am7
Dsus4
D
- ble
He said Roc-ky you met your match
And Roc-ky said, Doc it's on-ly a scratch
And I'll be
G7
bet-ter I'll be bet-ter doc as soon as I am a-ble
And now
Coda
da
D.S.

ROLL OVER BEETHOVEN

Words & Music by Chuck Berry.

G7
D7
G7
A7
D7
B
D7
G7
Well gon-na write a lit-tle let-ter Gon-na mail it to my lo-cal D. J.
tem-pera-ture's ris - in and the juke - box's blowin' a fuse
rock-in' pneu-mo - nia I need a shot of rhy-thm and blues
early in the mor-nin' I'm a giv-in' you the warn-in' Don't you
winks like a glow worm Dance like a spin - nin'
T
A
B
P

D7
G7
It's a rock-in' lit-tle rec-ord I want ___ my jock - ey to play _
My heart's ___ beat-in' rhy-thm and my soul keeps sing - ging the blues _
I think I got it off the writ-er sit-tin' down by the rhy-thm re-view _
step on my ___ blue suede shoes
Hey ___ lit-tle lit-tle gon-na play ___ my ___ fid-dle ___
top
She got a cra-zy part - ner ___ ought-a see ___ 'em ___ reel an rock _
T
A
B
D7
G7
A7
to
1.2.4.
D7
Roll o - ver Bee-tho-ven I got-ta hear it a-gain ___ to-day ___
Roll o - ver Bee-tho - ven ___ and tell Tchai-kow - sky the news ___
Roll o - ver Bee-tho - ven we-'re Rock-in' in two by two _
Ain't got noth-in' to lose ___
Roll o - ver Bee-tho - ven ___ and tell Tchai-kow - sky the news ___
Long as She's got a dime ___ the mu-sic will ___ ne - ver stop _

3.
C
D7
G7
You know my
I got a
You know She
Well if you feel you like it
Well get your lo - ver and
reel and rock it
roll it o-ver and
move on up just
jump around and
reel and rock it
roll it o-ver Roll o-
T
A
B

G7
D7
D
D7
- ver Bee-tho - ven a rock-in' in two by two oh
chop.
C
UD
G7
D7
G7
T
A
B

D7
G7
D7
h.c
chop.
h.u.
T
A
B
E
Well, _
Roll o - ver Bee - tho - ven
Roll o - ver Bee -
S
D.S.

D7
G7
D7
- tho - ven
Roll o - ver Bee - tho - ven
Roll o - ver Bee - tho - ven
Roll o - ver Bee -
A7
D7
- thoven and dig these rhy - thm and blues
h.c
Q.C
h.c
Q.C.

RUN FOR YOUR LIFE

Words & Music by John Lennon & Paul McCartney.

A
D
Bm
D
(1.4.) ra - ther see you dead, little girl than to be with a-no-ther man
(3.) know that I'm a wick - ed guy And I was born with a jea-lous mind
You be - tter keep your head, little girl or I
And I can't spend my whole life trying just to
(Aco. Guitar)
Bm
B
Bm
E
Bm
E
won't know where I am
make you toe the line
You bet-ter run for your life If you can li-ttle girl
Hide your head in the sand, li-ttle girl

Bm
G
F#7
1.
Bm
D
Catch you with a-no-ther man
That's the e - nd'a li-ttle girl
2.
Bm
D
Well you nd'a li-ttle girl
8va
Backing Guitar Simile
(Bottle Neck)

G
D
A
D
D
D
Bm
D
(3.) Let this be a ser - mon I mean eve - ry - thing I've said
Ba - by, I'm de-ter - mined And I'd
(8va)
(Aco. Guitar)

E
Bm
E
Bm
E
ra - ther see you dead__
You be-tter run for your life if you can,__ li-ttle girl__
Hide your head__ in the sand__ li-ttle girl__
Bm
G
F#7
Bm
D
Catch you with a - no - ther man__
That's the e - nd'a li-ttle girl
I'd
D.S.

Coda
Bm
F
D
- nd'a li-ttle girl
Na na na
na na na
na na na
na na na
(Bottle Neck)
Backing Guitar Simile
T
A
B
Fade Out

SAVOY TRUFFLE

Words & Music by George Harrison.

A
2.
E7
Upper Part 1 X Tacet
F#
A
a gin-ger sling ___ with a pine - ap-ple heart ___
I feel your taste ___ all the time ___ we're a-part ___
G
B
a cof-fee des-sert ___ yes, you know ___ it's good news. ___
Co-co-nut fudge ___ real-ly blows ___ down those blues. ___
But you'll
T
A
B
5 6 7
2 3 4
3 4 5
7 8 9

Em
C/E
Em6
C/E
C
to Φ 2.
1.
G
E7
have to have them all pulled out af-ter the Sa-voy truf - fle
1 x only
(2x)
(E. Piano)
2.
G
B
𝄋 1.
Em
Cool cher - ry cream (and a) nice ap-ple tart,
You might not feel it now,
know that what you eat you are,
(Organ)
8va bassa

A
Asus4
A
G
B
Em
A
but when the pain cuts through__ you're gon-na know, and how.__
The sweat is gon-na fill your head.____
when it be-
but what is sweet now__ turns so sour.__
We all know ob-la-di-bla-da,____
but can you
4.
Asus4
A
to ⊕ 1.
G
B
C
E7
- comes too much__ you'll shout a - loud__
show me__ where
B.G. Simile

E7
F#
A
G
UD
U
UD
H P
S
C D
B
D
Em
C
E
Em6
But you'll have to have them all pulled out ___ af - ter the Sa - voy ___ truf -
C
1 2 3

Coda 1.
C
G
B
E7
- fle
You
you are ?
Creme tan - ge-rine
and mon-tel-i-mar,
D.S. 1.
D.S. 2.
Coda 2.
G
Em
C/E
Em6
C/E
C
G
Yes, you'll have to have them all pulled out after the Sa-voy truf - fle

SEXY SADIE

Words & Music by John Lennon & Paul McCartney.

A (with Repeat)
G
F#7
Bm
C
D
(1x) Sexy Sadie
(2x) Sexy Sadie
(D.S.1x) Sexy Sadie
(D.S.2x) Sexy Sadie
what have you done
you broke the rules
how did you know
you'll get yours yet
You made a fool of everyone
You laid it down for all to see
The world was waiting just for you
However big you think you are
1x Tacet
D.S.X
(2x,DS2x)WA
(DS.1x)WA
WA
D.S.1X
(Arpeggio)
T
A
B
D.S.2x
2x
D.S.1X
You made a fool of everyone
You layed it down for all to see
The world was waiting just for you
However big you think you are
Sexy
Sexy
Sexy
Sexy
(1X, D.S.1X, D.S.2X) WA
(2x)See
D.S.1X

B
F
D7
G
Am7
Bm7
C△7
Sa - die o-oh what have you done
Sa - die o-oh you broke the rules One Sun-ny day the world was wait - ing for a lov-er
Sa - die o-oh how did you know
Sa - die o-oh you'll get yours yet We gave her eve-ry-thing we owned just to sit at her ta-ble
Se - xy Sa - die
(Organ)
2x
D.S.1x
D.S.x
A7
A♭△7
to ⊕
She came a-long to turn on eve-ry-one
Just a smile would light - en eve-ry-thing
Se-xy Sa - die the great-est of them all
Se-xy Sa-die she's the lat-est and the great-est of them all
Se-xy Sa-die She's the great - est
D.S.

Coda
C
Bm
1x only
G
F#7
C
D
Ha
Se-xy Sadie she's the latest and the greatest of them all
Organ
2x, 3x
h.c
1x, 2x
She made a fool of e-ve-ry-one
How ev-er big you think you are
Se-xy Sa-die
Se-xy Sa-die
F
D7
(2x)
Repeat & Fade Out

SGT. PEPPER'S LONELY HEARTS CLUB BAND

Words & Music by John Lennon & Paul McCartney.

A
G7
A7
C7
G7
G7
A7
twen-ty years a-go to-day
Ser-geant Pep-per taught the band to play
They've been go-ing in and out of style
but they're
real-ly want to stop the show
but I thought you might like to know
That the sing-er's going to sing a song
and he
C7
G7
A7
C7
gua-ran-teed to raise a smile
So may I in-tro-duce to you
the act you've known for all these years
wants you all to sing a-long
So may I in-tro-duce to you
the one and on-ly Bil-ly Shears
T
A
B

G7
C7
G7
to Φ
B
C7
F7
C7
Ser-geant Pep-per's Lone-ly Hearts Club Band
D7
C
G
Bb
C7
G
C7
We're Ser-geant Pep-per's Lone-ly Hearts Club Band We hope you will en-joy the show
C+D
C
C+D

G7
G
B♭
C7
G
A7
Ser - geant Pep - per's Lone - ly Hearts Club Band Sit back and let the eve - ning go
C
C+D
C
D7
D
C7
G7
A7
C7
Ser - geant Pep - per's Lone - ly Ser - geant Pep - per's Lone - ly Ser geant Pep - per's Lone - ly Hearts

C7
G7
E
F7
D7
Club Band
It's wonder-ful to be here it's cer-tain-ly a thrill
You're such a love-ly au-di-ence we'd
like to take you home with us we'd love to take you home
I don't
Coda
D.S.
Fade Out

SGT. PEPPER'S LONELY HEARTS CLUB BAND (REPRISE)

Words & Music by John Lennon & Paul McCartney.

A
F
A♭
B♭
F
B♭
We're Ser-geant Pepper's Lone - ly Hearts Club Band, We hope you will en-joy the show
F
F
A♭
B♭
F
G
C
Ser-geant Pep-per's Lone - ly Hearts Club Band We're so-rry but it's time to go
C+D

B♭
F
G
D
B
G
B♭
Ser-geant Pep-per's Lone - ly Ser - geant Pep-per's Lone - ly Ser - geant Pepper's Lone - ly Ser geant Pep-per's Lone - ly, Ser - geant Pep-per's Lone - ly Hearts
C
G
C
G
G
B♭
C
G
Club Band We'd like to thank you once a - gain
Ser-geant Pep-per's one and on - ly lone-ly Hearts Club Band It's

A
D
C
G
A
get-ting ve-ry near the end
Ser-geant Pep-per's Lone - ly Ser - geant Pep-per's Lone - ly Ser - geant Pep-per's Lone - ly Hearts
C
G
B♭
C
G
Club
Band
8va

SHE CAME IN THROUGH THE BATHROOM WINDOW

Words & Music by John Lennon & Paul McCartney.

D
Dsus4
A
F#m7
to Φ 1
- poon.
day.
job.
But now she sucks her thumb and won - ders
And though she thought I knew the ans - wer ;
And though she tried her best to help me ,
By the banks of her own la-goon
Well, I knew what I could not say
She could steal, but she could not rob,
Ooo
Ah
B
Dm
Didn't a - ny - bod - y tell her ?
Didn't a - ny - bod - y see ?
(with Tambourine)

G7
C
G
B
G7
to ⊕ 2.
C
A
Sun-day's on the phone to Mon - day ;
Tues-day's on the phone to me,
⊕ Coda 1.
A
⊕ Coda 2.
C
A
She said she'd al - ways been a dan-
And so I quit the Police De-part-
Oh, yeah.
Ah
D.S. 1.
D.S. 2.

SHE LOVES YOU

Words & Music by John Lennon & Paul McCartney.

C
G
𝄋 (Straight)
A
G
Em7
Bm
yeah, yeah, yeah!
You (1) think you've lost your love,
(2) said you hurt her so,
(3) know it's up to you,
Well, I saw her yes - ter -
She al - most lost her
I think it's on - ly
T.C.
D7
G
Em7
Bm
D7
- day - yi - yay.
mind,
fair,
It's you she's think - ing of,
And now she says she knows
Pride can hurt you too,
And she told me what to say - yi - yay.
You're not the hurt - ing kind.
A - pol - o - gize to her.
She says she
She says she
Be-cause she

B
G
Em
Cm
loves you. and you know that can't be bad.
Yes, she loves you, and you know you should be glad.
1.
D7
2.
She
Oo
C
Em
She loves you, yeah, yeah, yeah, she

A7
Cm
D7
to Coda G
loves you, yeah yeah, yeah, And with a love like that you know you should be glad.
You
D.S.
Coda
G
Em
Cm
D7
G
And with a love like that you know you should be glad.

Em
Cm
D7
D
G
And with a love like that you know you should be glad
Em♭
C
G♭
Yeah, yeah, yeah, Yeah, yeah, yeah, yeah.

SHE SAID SHE SAID

Words & Music by John Lennon & Paul McCartney.

E♭
B♭7
A♭
I know what it's like to be dead
Who put all those things in your head
E - ven though you know what you know
I know what it is to be sad
Things that make me feel that I'm mad
I know that I'm rea - dy to leave
And she's mak-ing me feel like I've ne-ver been born
And you're mak-ing me feel like I've ne-ver been born
'cause you're mak-ing me feel like I've ne-ver been born
1.

2.3.
E♭
B♭7
B
B♭7
A♭7
B♭7
A♭7
She said you don't un-der-stand what I said I said no, no, no you're
B♭7
Fm
B♭7
E♭
B♭7
wrong When I was a boy
Eve-ry-thing was right,

B♭7
E♭
4.
B♭7
C B♭7
She said
ev'-ry-thing was right
She said
I know what it's
C
H
S
I know what it's like to be dead
I know what it is to be said
like to be dead
I know what it is to be sad
I know what it's like to be dead
I know what it's
Fade Out

SHE'S A WOMAN

Words & Music by John Lennon & Paul McCartney.

A
A7
A7
D7
A7
(1.3.) My love don't give me pres - ents,
(2.4.) She don't give boys the eye,
1X Tacet
H.H.
(with Maracas)
A7
D7
A7
I know that she's no peas - ant,
She hates to see me cry,
4.

D7
A7
On - ly ev - er has___ to give___ me Love for - ev - er and for - ev - er, My___ love___ don't
She is hap - py just___ to hear___ me Say that I will nev - er leave her, She___ don't___ give
D7
A7
E7
give me pres - ents.
boys the eyes.___
Turn me on___ when I___ get lone - ly,
She will nev - er make___ me jeal - ous,

to ⊕
1.
D7
A7
D7
A7
People tell me that she's only foolin', I know she isn't
Gives me all her time as well as lovin', Don't ask me why
E7
2.
A7
B
C#m
F#
She's a woman who understands,
T
A
B
10 11 12 13
5 6 7 8
12 13 14 15
4 5 6
2 3 4
H
T.C~

C#m
D
E
3.
A7
E7
C
A7
She's a wo - man who loves her man;
Woo oo oo Woo
D7

A7
E7
D7
A7
E7
D
C#m
F#
C#m
D
E
She's a wo - man who un - der - stands,
She's a wo - man who loves her man;
T.C
D.S.

Coda
E
A7
A7
She's a wo - man,
She's a wo-man,
She's a
D7
A7
E7
wo - man,
She's a wo-man,
She's a wo - man,
T.C.~
Fade Out

SHE'S LEAVING HOME

Words & Music by John Lennon & Paul McCartney.

F#m7
C#m7
F#7
five o'-clock as the day be-gins
B7sus4
B9
B7sus4
Sil - ent - ly clos - ing her bed - room door
Leav - ing the note that she

B
B9
E
Bm
F#m7
hoped would say more She goes down stairs to the kit - chen clutch - ing her
C#m
F#7
B7sus4
hand - ker-chief
Qui-et - ly turn - ing the back_

B9
B7sus4
B9
B7
door key
Step-ing out - side she is free
E
C
She
is leav - ing
We gave her most of our lives
Sac - ri - ficed
4
4

Home
Bm6
most of our lives
We gave her ev'-ry-thing money could
C#m
She's leav-ing home af-ter
F#7
liv-ing a-lone for so
C#m
ma-ny years
buy
Bye
bye

F#7
D
E
Bm
F#m7
C#m7
Fa - ther snores as his wife gets in - to her dres-sing gown
F#7
B7sus4
B9
Picks up the let - ter that's ly - ing there

B9
B7sus4
B9
E
E
Stand - ing a - lone at the top of the stairs She breaks down and
Bm
F#m7
C#m
F#7
cries to her hus - band Dad-dy our ba - by's gone
T
A
B

F#7
B7sus4
B9
B7sus4
Why would she treat us so thought - less - ly
How could she do this to me
B9
B7
F
E
She
We ne - ver thought of our
T
A
B

is leav - ing
Home
- selves
nev - er a thought for our - selves
4
4
Bmb
C#m
F#7
She's leav - ing home af - ter liv-ing a -
We strug-gled hard all our lives to get by

F#7
C#m
G
F#7
E
Bm
-lone for so many - y years
Bye bye
Fri - day morn - ing at
F#m7
C#m
F#7
nine o'-clock she is far a-way
T
A
B

B7sus4
B9
B7sus4
Wait - ing to keep the ap-point - ment she made
Meet - ing a man from the
tr
tr
B9
B7
H
She
is
mo - tor trade
What did we do that was wrong
T
A
B

E
hav - ing
Fun
We did-n't know it was wrong
Fun is the
Bm6
C#m
F#7
some - thing in - side that was al - ways de-nied for so
one thing that mo-ney can't buy
Bye

C#m7
man - y years
bye
F#7
C#m
She's leav - ing
4
F#7
home
Bye
A
bye
E

SLOW DOWN

Words & Music by Larry Williams.

C
F
S
P
S
T
A
B
1214
13
15
12
14
7
8
1 2 3 4
10
C
G
9
79
10
1012
8 9 10 11
3 4 5 6

G
F
C
A
(D.S.X)
C
Well, come on, pret - ty ba - by, won't you walk with me? Come on, pret - ty ba - by won't you
used to walk you home, ba - by, af - ter school. Car - ry your books home, too
know that I love you, tell the world I do; Come on, pret - ty ba - by, why can't

C
talk with me?
Come on, pret - ty ba - by, give me one more Chance.
Try and save
But now you got a boy - friend down the street,
Ba - by what're you tryin' to do a
you be true?
I need you bad - ly, ba - by, oh so bad,
The best lit - tle wo - man I
B
F
our ro - mance! Slow down!
do? You bet - ter slow down!
ev - er had, Slow down!
Ba - by, now you're
1x, 3x Snare Dr.

F
C
mov - in' way too fast.
You got - ta
G
F
C
gim-me lit-tle lov - in', gim-me lit-tle lov - in',
Ow! Brrr! Ow!
if you want our love to last.
1×

C
to
1.
2.
C
C
C
Well, I
B.G. Simile
D.S.

C
F
S
S
H.C
H.U D
H
H.C.
H.C
1 2 3 4
P
P
C
G
H.C
H.U
H.U
D
H.U D
1 2 3
3 4 5 6

G
F
C
H.U.D
S
P
1 2 3 4
1 2 3
Coda
C
Well, you
H.C
H.U
H
D.S.

SOMETHING

Words & Music by George Harrison.

D7
G
Am
AmΔ7
Am7/G
D9
to Φ
Some-thing in the way, she woos me
Some-thing in her style, that shows me
Some-thing in the things, she shows me
I don't want to leave her now
You know I be-lieve and how.
1 x only
(E.G.)
(Organ)
1.
F
E♭
G/D
2.
F
E♭
G/D
A
B
A
C♯m/G♯
You're ask-ing me will my love
hu D P
(Organ)
(E.Guitar)

F#m7
A/E
D
G
A
A
C#m/G#
F#m7
A/E
grow
I don't know
I
don't know
You stick a-round_ and it may show
I don't know_
D
G
C
C
C
CΔ7
C7
I
don't know
H
C
UD
S
Cym.

F
D
G7
Am
AmΔ7
Am7
D9
(E.G)
(Organ)
Coda
Eb
G/D
A
C
8va.
(Organ)
H.H.
Cym.
D.S.

STRAWBERRY FIELDS FOREVER

Words & Music by John Lennon & Paul McCartney.

B♭
Fm7
G7
— cause I'm go-in' to straw-be-rry fields
Noth-ing is real and
(Guitar II)
(1x only)
(D.S.1x D.S.2x)
(D.S.2x)
(1x only)
Bass (1x only)
Contrabass (2x D.S.1x D.S.2x)
(Dubbing Bass Tom) (2x D.S.1x D.S.2x)
E♭
G7
E♭
B♭
F
to ⊕ (D.S.2x)
1.
B 𝄋 1. (with Repeat) 2. (with Repeat)
noth-ing to get hung a-bout
Straw-be-rry fields for - e-ver
Liv - ing is ea - sy with
No one I think is in
Al - ways know some -
(Brass Section) 2x, D.S.1x, D.S.2x
(D.S.1x D.S.2x)
(1x only)
Bass 1x only

F7
Gm
Gm7
F
E♭
E♭
F
eyes closed
my tree
-times it's me
Mis-un-der-stand-ing all you see
I mean it must be high or low
But you know I know when it's a dream
It's get-ting hard to be some-
That is you know you can't tune
I think a "No" will mean a
(D.S.1x)
Contra bass (2x, D.S.1x, D.S.2x)
B♭
Gm
E♭
F
E♭
B♭
2.3.
B♭
-one but it all works out
in but it's all right
"Yes," but it's all wrong
It does-n't mat-ter much to me
that is I think it's not too bad
that is I think I dis-ag-ree
-e-ver
(Sitar)
(D.S.1x)
(D.S.2x)
(Contra bass)
D.S. 1. 2.

Coda
B♭
E♭
B♭
E♭
F
E♭
- e-ver
Straw-be-rry fields_ for - e- ver
straw-be- rry fields_ for - e-ver
U D
H P
(Piano)
(Contra bass)
(Dubbing Bass Drum)
C
B♭
B♭/A♭
B♭/A♭
B♭
B♭
tr.

B♭
(Sitar)
D
N.C.
(Tape Reverse)
Fade Out
Fade In

N.C.
w.h.c
w.h.c
(Piano)
Dubbing Bass Drum
Fade Out

SUN KING

Words & Music by John Lennon & Paul McCartney.

F#m7
E
D.S.x only
E6
Quan-do para mu-cho mi a-mor-e de-fe-li-ce cor-a-zon
F#m7
E
Mun-do pa-pa-raz-zi mi a-
1x only
1x only
-mor-e chick a fer-dy pa-ra-sol
E6
F#m7
E
to ⊕
Cue-sto ob-ri-ga-do tan-ta mu-cho que can eat it car-ou-

E6
F
G
B
C
CΔ7
Ah
Here
comes
the
Gm7
A7
C
CΔ7
Gm7
A7
Sun
King
Here
comes
the
Sun
King

C
F
D7
F
D7
D C
Ev - 'ry - bod - y's laugh - ing
Ev - 'ry - bod - y's hap - py
Here
Em7
C7
F
comes the Sun King.
Coda
E6
sel.
D.S.

A TASTE OF HONEY

Words by Ric Marlow. Music by Bobby Scott.

B
F#m
F#mΔ7
F#7
B
F#m
them I feel u - pon my lips a - gain A taste of ho-ney a taste of
heart There ling - ers still tho we're far a - part The taste of ho-ney a taste of
A
E
F#m
B
F#m
ho-ney
ho-ney
Tast - ing much sweet - er than wine
F#m
B
F#m
B
F#m
B
F#m
I will re - turn yes I will re-turn

B
to
A
E
F#m
I'll come back For the ho-ney and you Do dut don du
to dut don du Yours
Coda
Tempo Rubato
A
E
back I'll come back for the ho-ney for the
D.S.
In Tempo
F#m
B
F#m
F#m
F#m
ho-ney And you

TAXMAN

Words & Music by George Harrison.

D7+9
D7
D7
D7+9
D7
There's one for you, nine teen for me
Be thank - ful I don't take it all
If you don't want to pay some more
Dec-lare the pen - nies on your eyes
(4x) Tax - man
(3x) Ha ha Mis-ter Wilson
(4x) Tax - man
(3x) Ha ha Mis-ter Heath
4.
B
C
G7
to
'cause I'm the tax - man,
yeah I'm the Tax - man
yeah I'm the Tax - man
Q.C

1.
2.
C
D7
Should five
Now my
D7
D7
I'll tax the street
If you drive a car car
If you try
1X, 2X Tacet
(4X Simile)
C7
D7
I'll tax your seat
I'll tax the heat
I'll tax
to sit sit
If you get too cold cold
If you take a walk walk

D
C7
D7
your feet
Tax - man
Tax - man
D7+9
D7

D7+9
E
C
'cause I'm the Tax - man
Yeah I'm the
Yeah I'm the
Q.C
4.
G7
D7
Tax - man
Don't ask
Tax - man
Coda
D7
And you're
D.S.

F
F7
D7
D7+9
working For no one but me
Tax - man
Fade Out

TELL ME WHAT YOU SEE

Words & Music by John Lennon & Paul McCartney.

G
C
G
G
C
D
G
I will prove to you
Time will pass a - way
How can I get through
We will ne - ver be a - part
If you put your trust in me
Can't you try to see that I'm
1x only
D.S. 1x
C
D
G
B
C
G
If I'm part of you
I'll make bright your day
Tryin' to get to you
O - pen up your eyes now
Look in - to these eyes now
O - pen up your eyes now
2x
D.S. 2x

C
G
C
G
Tell me what you see
It is no surprise now
Tell me what you see
Don't you re - a - lize now
Tell me what you see
It is no sur - prise now
D.S.2x
D.S.2x
D.S.2x
D.S.2x
C
D
G
C G7add9
What you see is me
What you see is me
What you see is me
(1x, 2x) Tell me what you
(3x) mm mm mm mm
1x D.S.1x
D.S.1x
D.S.2x
D.S.2x
D.S.2x

C
(Electric Piano)
G
D7
G
see
D.S.1×
1×only
1 2 3
D.S.1×
(S.D)
(Rim)
(Ele.pf)
Coda
C
(Electric Piano)
rit.
G
mm
D.S. 1. 2.

TELL ME WHY

Words & Music by John Lennon & Paul McCartney.

Bm7
Em7
A7
D6
D6/B
Em7
A7
you cried
And why you lied to me
Tell me
D
Bm7
Em7
A7
to
D6
1x 2x (B)
why
you cried
And why you lied to me
S.D.2x
S.D.3x

1. 2.
Em7
A7
B
D
Bm7
Em7
Well I gave you ev'-ry-thing I had
But you left me sit-ting on my own
If there's some-thing I have said or done
Tell me what and I'll ap-ol-o-gize
A7
D
Bm7
Em7
Did you have to treat me oh so bad
All I do is hang my head and moan
If you don't I real-ly can't go on
Hold-ing back these tear in my eyes
2x S.D.

A7
3.
D7
C G7
Tell me
Well I beg you on my ben-ded knees
If you'll
A7
Bm
on-ly lis-ten to my pleas
Is there a-ny-thing I can do
'cause I

Em7
A7
D
real-ly can't stand it I'm so in love with you
Tell me
D.S.
Coda
Bm
B♭7
A7(11)
A7(13)
D
me

THANK YOU GIRL

Words & Music by John Lennon & Paul McCartney.

D G D A7 D G D G D G D A7
me; you made me glad when I was blue. And e-ter-nal-ly I'll al-ways be in love with
world a thing or two a-bout our love. I know lit-tle girl on-ly a fool would doubt our
D G A7 G to Φ 1. A7 2. A7
you. love. And all I got-ta do is thank you girl. Thank you girl. Thank you girl.

B
Bm
D
A7
Em
A7
Thank you girl for lov - in' me the way that you do. (Way that you do.) That's the kind of love that is too
D
G
A7
G
A7
good to be true. And all I got - ta do is thank you girl.__ Thank you girl.__
D.C.

Coda
A7
G
C
A7
Thank you girl.
Ah
Mute
G
1.2.
D
G
D
G
3.
D
Ah
Ah
Mute

THERE'S A PLACE

Words & Music by John Lennon & Paul McCartney.

A
(Straight)
E
A
E
A
E
C#m
(1.3.) place
where I can go
When I feel low
when I feel
(2.) you
the things you do
Go round my head
the things you've
B
1.
B
G#m
A
E
A
blue
And it's my mind
and there's time
When I'm a -
said

C#m
to ⊕
2.
C
B
A
-lone
I
think of
Like I love
o-n-ly
(Chorus)
Ah
B
D
C#m
F#m
E
you
in my mind there's no sor-row
Don't you know that it's
Ah

G#
C#m
F#m
E
G#
so
There'll be no sad to - mo-rrow
Don't you know that it's so
C#m
There
there's a
Coda
E
C#m
E
A
There's a place
there's a
D.S.
Repeat & Fade Out

THINGS WE SAID TODAY

Words & Music by John Lennon & Paul McCartney.

Am
Em7
Am
Em7
Am
Am
Em7
if I have to go
'til the end of time
be-lieve on-ly one
You'll be think-ing of me
These days such a kind girl
loves me all a time girl
some-how I will know
Seems so hard to find
we'll go on and on
D.S.2x only
2x
D.S.1x
D.S.2x
2x
D.S.1x, D.S.2x
B
C
C9
F
B♭
Some-day when I'm lone-ly
wish-ing you weren't so far a-way
Some-day when we're dream-ing
deep in love not a lot to say

to Φ
1.
Am
Em7
Am
Am
Em7
Am
Then I will re - mem - ber
Then we will re - mem - ber
Then we will re - mem - ber
1X, DS1 Tacet
Things we said to - day
Things we said to - day
Things we said to - day
1x only
Guitar III
1X, D.S.2X
1X, D.S.2X
1 2 3
(Tambourine)
2.
A
C
A
D7
B7
Me I'm just the luc - ky kind
Love to hear you say
D.S. 2X
H.H. open

E7
A
D7
B7
that love is love And though we may - be blind Love is here to stay
D.S.1x
B♭7
Coda
Am
and that's en - ough
Guitar III
H.H. Open
D.S. 1. 2. al Coda
(Tambourine)
Repeat & Fade Out

THINK FOR YOURSELF

Words & Music by George Harrison.

B♭
C
G7
To say a - bout the things that you do
The ru - ins of the life that you had in mind
Try think - ing more if just for your own sake
Am
Dm
B♭
C
You're tell - ing all those lies
A - bout the good things that we can
And though you still can't see
I know your mind's made up You 're
The fu - ture still looks good
And you've got time to rec - ti - fy

G7
Am
B
C7
have if we close our eyes
gon - na cause more mise - ry
All the things that you should
Do what you want to do
And
G7
Eb/Bb
D7
go where you're go - ing to
Think for your- self 'cause I won't be there with you

1. 2. 3.
4.
G7
G7
C
C7
G7
Do what you want to do
And go where you're go - ing to
P
P

Eb/Bb
D7
C7
G7
Think for your- self 'cause I won't be there with you
D Eb/Bb
D7
C7
G7
Think for your- self 'cause I won't be there with you

THIS BOY

Words & Music by John Lennon & Paul McCartney.

Em
A7
D
Bm
took my love a - way.
is - n't good for you,
Oh, he'll re-gret it some day,
Though he may want you too
Em/D
But this boy wants you back a-
This boy wants you back a-
1.
gain.
2.
Dsus4
D9
On, and

B
G
F#7
Bm
D7
G
Ah
this boy would be hap-py just to love you But oh, my! oh That boy won't be
E7
A7
C
D
Bm
Em
A7
hap-py till he's seen you cry This boy would-n't mind the
1 2 3
2 3 4 5
2 3 4
1 2 3
1 2 3

D Bm Em A7 D Bm Em D A7 D Bm
pain, Would al-ways feel the same, if this boy gets you back a-gain.
Em A7 D D7 Bm Em A7 D Bm Em A7
This boy, this boy.
Repeat & Fade Out

TICKET TO RIDE

Words & Music by John Lennon & Paul McCartney.

A
I think it's to-day
is bring-ing her down
Yeah!
Yeah!
The girl that's driv-ing me mad
For she would ne-ver be free
is go-ing a-way
when I was a-round
Bm
E
D.S.1x (Yeah
oh!)
D.S.2x (oh!)
F#m
D7
She's got a tic-ket to ride

F#m
G△7
F#m
E
She's got a tic-ket to ride
She's got a tic-ket to ride
but she don't care
A
to
1.
2.
B D7
She
I don't know why she's rid-ing so high

D7
E
E7
D7
She ought to think right she ought to do right by me
Be - fore she gets to say - ing good-bye
E
She ought to think right she ought to do right by me
She
D.S.1×(
D.S. 1.
2. al Coda

Coda
A
C A
My ba - by don't care
My ba - by don't care
My ba - by don't
care
My ba - by don't care
My ba - by don't care
Hand Clap
hc & D
C & D
hc
c
Fade Out

TILL THERE WAS YOU

Words & Music by Meredith Willson.

F#dim
Gm7
B♭m7
F
Am7
A♭m7
Gm7
Gm7/C
hill
But I ne-ver heard them ring-ing
No I ne-ver heard them at all
Till
But I ne-ver saw them win-ging
No I ne ver saw them at all
Till
1.
2.
B
F
Gm7
Gm7/C
F
F9
B♭
there was you
There were there was you
Then there was mu - sic

D.S.
B♭m
F
D9
Gm7
GmΔ7
G7
and wonderful Ro - ses they tell me in sweet fra-grant mea-dows of
C
Gm7/C
Caug
C
F
F♯dim
Gm7
dawn and dew
there was love
there was love
all a - round But I ne-ver heard it
(Acoustic Guitar)
D.S.

B♭m7
F
Am7
A♭m7
Gm7
Gm7/C
F
to Φ
Gm7
Gm7/C
sin-ging
No___ I___ ne-ver heard it at all
Till there was you___
(Gut Guitar)
D.S.
D
F
F♯dim
Gm7
B♭m7
F
Am7
A♭m7

Gm7
G♭7 -10 -5
F
F7 -9
Then there was
Coda
F
C
B
Till
D.S.
C
F
D♭9
F
F
F△7
there was you

TOMORROW NEVER KNOWS

Words & Music by John Lennon & Paul McCartney.

A
C
(5.) ig - nor - rance and hate May mourn the dead
(6.) lis - ten to the co - lour of your dreams
(7.) play the game ex - is - tance to the end
(with 3 times Repeat)
off you mind, re - lax And float down stream
(2) down all thought Sur - ren - der to the void
(3.) you may see The mean - ing of with in
(4.) love is all And love is eve - ry one
B♭/C
It is be - lieving
It is not living
Of the begin - ning
It is not dying
It is shin - ing
It is be - ing
It is know - ing
(Organ)
C
to
1.2.
3.
C
(2.) Lay
(3.5.) That
(6.) But
(7.) Or
B
C
(S.E. Solo)

C
T
A
B
h.c D

C
That
D.S.
Coda
C
B♭
C
C
Of the begin - ning
Of the begin - ning

1.
C
2.
C
B♭
C
Of the begin -
Of the begin - ning
(Piano)
T
A
B
Fade Out

TWIST AND SHOUT

Words & Music by Bert Russell & Phil Medley.

B
D G A7
1.) - by, now
2.) - by, now
3.) - by, now
Twist and shout.
Come on, come on, come on, come on, ba-by now,
Shake it up ba - by
Twist and shout
Come on ba - by
T
A
B
(T.C.)
D G A7
C
Come on and work it on out,
1.) Well, work it on out, hon - ey
2.3.) You know you twist, lit-tle girl,
You know you look so
You know you twist so
Work it on out
Woo
Work it on out
Twist lit - tle girl

D G A7 D G to⊕ A7 1.
good. You know you got me go - in' now, Just like I knew you would.
fine. Come on and twist a lit - tle clo - ser now,
Look so good
Twist so fine
Got me go - in'
Twist a lit-tle clo-
D G A7 2. A7 D G A7
Well, shake it up ba- And let me know that you're mine
Like I knew you would Woo - er Let me know you're mine

A7
D
D
G
A7
A7
D
G
A7
A7
Woo
Woo
(H. H.)
D
G
A7
A7
D
G
A7
A7
E
A
Ah
(T.C.)

A
Wow! Wow! Yeah! shake it up ba-
Ah Ah Ah
D.S.
Coda
A7 D G A7 A7 D G A7
And let me know that you're mine
Well, shake it, shake it, shake it, ba-by, now.
Well, shake it, shake it, shake it,
-er
Let me know you're mine
Woo
Shake it up, ba-by

D
G
A7
A7
D
G
A7
A7
ba - by, now.
Well, shake it, shake it, shake it, ba - by now.
Shake it up, ba - by
Shake it up, ba - by
F
A
A
D9
Ah
Ah
Ah

TWO OF US

Words & Music by John Lennon & Paul McCartney.

A
1. 2. (Straight)
G
C
C/B
Am7
(1) Two of us rid - ing no - where spend - ing some - one's hard - earned pay.
(2) Two of us send - ing post - cards writ - ing let - ters on my wall.
(3.4.) Two of us wear - ing rain - coats stand - ing so - lo in the sun.
You and me Sun - day driv - ing not ar - riv - ing
You and me burn - ing match - es lift - ing latch - es
You and me chas - ing pa - per get - ting no - where

C
C
B
Am7
G
D
C
on our way back home we're on our way
on our way back home we're on our way
G
D
C
G
C
(D.S.2x)
to
1.
G
home we're on our way home we're go - ing home
home we're on our way home we're go - ing home

2.
G
B
B♭
Dm
home
You and I ___ have me - mo - ries
home
Gm7
Am
D7
long - er than ___ that road ___ that stretches ___ out ___ a - head
out ahead
D.S. 1. 2.

Coda
G
C
G
home
We're going home.
home
D (Whistle)
Repeat & Fade Out

WAIT

Words & Music by John Lennon & Paul McCartney.

F#m7
F#m6
Bm/F#
F#m
C#7
F#m
B
A6
- way now Oh, how I've been a - lone
heart's strong Hold on, I won't de - lay
Wait till I
come back to your side
A6
C#7
1.
F#m
We'll for - get the tears we've cried
But if your
1x tacet
(Tambourine)

2.3
F#m
C B
E
A
I feel as though You ought to know That I've been good As good as I can
3x only
3x only
3x S.D. & B.T. only
F#m
B
E
A
be And if you do I'll trust in you And know that you will wait for
3x
3x

C#7
4.
F#m
D
F#m7
F#m6
Bm/F#
F#m
C#7
me It's been a (4.) it's been a long time Now I'm coming back home I've been a -
(T.C.)
F#m7
F#m6
Bm/F#
F#m
C#7
F#m
- way now Oh, how I've been a - lone

WE CAN WORK IT OUT

Words & Music by John Lennon & Paul McCartney.

D
C
D
G
D
G
A7
B
D
Run the risk of know-ing that our love may soon be gone.
We can work it out.
We can work it out.
Think of what you're say - ing,
Try to see it my way,

C
D
You can get it wrong and still you think that it's all right.
On-ly time will tell if I am right or I am wrong.
Think of what I'm say - ing.
While you see it your way.
We can work it out and get it
There's a chance that we might fall a -

C
D
to
G
D
G
A7
C
Bm
straight, or say good night.
- part be-fore too long.
We can work it out.
We can work it out.
Life is ver- y short,
and there's no time
(2 x Arpeggio)
G
F#
Bm
Bm
for fuss-ing and fight-ing, my friend.
I have al-ways thought
that it's a crime,
(2x)

G
F#
Bm
1.
D7
2.
D7
So I will ask you once a - gain.
-gain.
D.S.
Coda
G
D
G
A7
D
We can work it out.
We can work it out.

WHAT GOES ON?

Words & Music by John Lennon, Paul McCartney & Richard Starkey.

E7
A7
E7
what goes on
in your mind ?
You are tear - - ing me a-part
A7
B7
to
When you treat me so un-kind
What goes on
in your mind

E7
B
E7
Am
(1) The o-ther day I saw you As I walk-eda-long the road But
(2) I met you in the morn-ing wait-ing for the tides of time But
Woo
Woo
Simile
Simile
E7
Am
Am
B7
when I saw him with you I could feel my fu-ture fold
now the tide is turn-ing I can see that I was blind
It's so ea-sy for a girl like you to lie
Woo
Woo
Woo
Woo

E7
B7
E7
C
E7
Tell me why
What goes on
in your heart
What goes on
in your heart
A7
E7

E7
A7
B7
E7
(3) I
D
E7
Am
E7
used to think of no - one else But you were just the same You did-n't e - ven think of me As
Woo
Woo
Woo

Am
Am
B7
E7
B7
some - one with a name
Did you mean to break my heart and watch me die
Tell me why
What goes on
Woo
Woo
Woo
Woo
What goes on
D.S.
Coda
E7
in your mind
in your mind

WHAT YOU'RE DOING

Words & Music by John Lennon & Paul McCartney.

D
G
A
D
G
D
Look What You're Do-ing I'm feel-ing
You got me run-ning and there's no
G
Bm
G
D
(woo)
blue and lone-ly would it be too much to ask of you What You're Do-ing to me
fun in it why should it

1.
G
2.
G
B
Bm
G
Bm
I've been waiting here for you
won - d'ring what you're gon-na do
E
A
C
D
should you need a love that's true it's me
Please stop your

G D G Bm G
(woo
ly-ing you got me cry-ing girl why should it be so much to ask of you What You're
)
to D G D D G7
Do-ing to me
T
A
B
1 2 3
2 3 4

D
G7
Bm7
G7
D
G
I've been waiting
D.S.
Coda
D
G
me
What You're Do - ing
to

D
G
D
G
D
me
What You're Do - ing
to
me
A
D
G7
Repeat & Fade Out

WHEN I GET HOME

Words & Music by John Lennon & Paul McCartney.

D7
G7
2×
Am
G7
whole lot of things to tell her
when I get home
Come
2×
5 6 7
3 4 5 6
1 2 3
3 4 5
5 6 7
3 4 5
5 6 7
3 4 5
(Straight)
B C7
F7
2× D.S.×
C7
F7
(1×) on
I'm on my way
'cause I'm a gon-na see my ba - by to - day
I've got a
(2×) on
if you please
I've got no time for triv - i - al - it - ies
I've got a
(3×) on
let me through
I got so ma - ny things I got - ta do
I got
1 2 3
1 2 3 4
3 4 5
1 2 3

C
F7
G7
whole lot of things I've got - ta say to her
girl who's wait - ing home for me to - night
no busi - ness be - ing here with you this way
Whoa ah
D.S.x
2x, D.S.x
C
A7
Whoa ah
D7
I got a whole lot of things to tell her

G7
DS×
to
Am
D C
when I get home
When I'm get-ting home to-night I'm gon-na
Am
C
Am
F
hold her tight I'm gon-na love her till the cows come home
I bet I'll love her more

G7
F
G7
Am
G7
till I walk out that door again come
D.S.

Coda
A7
D7
G7
C
Yeah I've got a whole lot of things to tell her when I get home

WHEN I'M SIXTY FOUR

Words & Music by John Lennon & Paul McCartney.

A
C
G7
When I get old - er losing my hair___ ma - ny years from now___ will you still be send-ing me a
I could be hand - dy mend-ing a fuse___ when your lights have gone,___ you can knit a sweat - er by the
C
va - len - tine,___ birth - day greet - ing, bot-tle of wine___ If I'd been out___ till quar-ter to three___
fi - re - side,___ Sun - day morn - ings, go for a ride___ do-ing the gar - den dig-ging the weeds___
2x only
T
A
B

C7
F
Fm
C
A
D
G7
would you lock the door
will you still need me,
will you still feed me,
when I'm sixty-four
Who could ask for more
will you still need me,
will you still feed me,
when I'm sixty-four
T
A
B
C
B
Am
G
Am
(1X Tacet)
(2X) Ev'-ry sum-mer we can rent a cot-tage in the Isle of Wight if it's not too dear
(1x chorus 2x Tacet)
2x Tacet
Oo

Am
E
Am
You'll be old - er too
We shall scrimp and save
And if you
Grand child - ren
Ah
we shall scrimp and save
Ah
Ah
Chorus
Dm
Em
F
G
C
G
say the word
on your knee
I could stay with you
Ve - ra, Chuck and Dave
Bell
2x

G
C
C
G7
Bell
Send me a post - card drop me a line___ stat-ing point of view,___
in - di-cate pre-cise-ly what you mean to say___ yours sin - cere - ly wast-ing a-way___ Give me your an - swer
C

C
F
Fm
C
A
fill in a form
mine for-ev-er more
Will you still need me,
will you still feed me
D
G7
C
D
C
F
G
C
when I'm six-ty-four
T
A
B

WHILE MY GUITAR GENTLY WEEPS

Words & Music by George Harrison.

D
E
A
Am
(1x upper part tacet)
Am
G
D9
F#
I look at you all see the love there that's sleep-
at the world and I no - tice it's turn-
at you all see the love there that's sleep-
(Perc)
(1x tacet)
FΔ7
(1x tacet)
Am
G
D
E
ing while my Gui-tar gent-ly weeps I look
- ing while my Gui-tar gent-ly weeps With eve-
- ing while my Gui-tar gent-ly weeps
D.S.x

B
Am
Am/G
D9/F#
FΔ7
Am (D.S. only upper part)
at the floor and I see it needs sweep - ing
ry mis - take we must sure - ly be learn - ing
I look at you all
Still my gui-tar
Still my gui-tar
Still my gui-tar
G
(D.S. only)
to
1.
C
E
(with Repeat)
C
A
C#m
gent - ly weeps
gent - ly weeps
gent - ly weeps
I don't know why
I don't know how
(Organ)
(Piano)
D.S.x Tambourine
(D.S.x Tambourine)
8va
h.c

F#m
C#m
Bm
E
no - bo - dy told you how to un - fold your love
you were di - ver - ted you were per - ver - ted too
A
C#m
F#m
C#m
I don't know how some - one con - trolled you
I don't know how you were in - ver - ted

Bm
E
2.
C
they bought and sold you
no one alt - er - ed you
I look
I look
yeah
E
D Am
Am
G
D9
F#
FΔ7
Am
ah
vib & D
S.D
Tom

G
D
E
Am
Am/G
D9/F#
F∆7
Am
G
C
E
8va.
Tambourine
D.S.

Coda
C
E
E
Am
Am
G
D9
F#
FΔ7
oh
oh
(Organ)
(Piano)
Am
G
D
E
Am
Am
G
oh
oh
oh
oh
oh
oh
gliss.
(Tambou-rine)

D9/F#
F∆7
Am
G
C
E
oh
oh
F
Am
Am/G
D9/F#
F∆7
Am
G
oh
oh
oh
oh
oh
oh
8va

D
E
Am
Am/G
D9/F#
Yeah Yeah Yeah Yeah Yeah Yeah Yeah Yeah
8va
FΔ7
Am
G
C
E
Fade Out

WHY DON'T WE DO IT IN THE ROAD?

Words & Music by John Lennon & Paul McCartney.

(3 times)
A
D7
3x
Why don't we do it in the road
Ah
Why don't we do— it in— the road—
3x(— it do it in the—)
1x tacet.
(Arpe-ggio)
(Top)
G7
wu
Why don't we do— it in the road
1x tacet
D7

D7
A7
1. 2.
G7
No one will be wat - ching us Why don't we do it in the road
D7
8va
3.
G7
D7
oh why don't we do it in the road why don't we do it in the road
(H.H)
(H.H. Open)

WILD HONEY PIE

Words & Music by John Lennon & Paul McCartney.

G7
vib.
vib.
B
G7
F7
Ho - ney Pie
Ho - ney Pie
8va
E7
E♭7
D7
G7
C
G7
Ho - ney Pie
Ho - ney Pie
8va
(Guitar II B 1～2 Call)
Guitar III → (8va)

F7
E7
E♭7
D7
G7
Ho - ney Pie
8va
(Guitar III)
F7
G7
F7
G7
Ho - ney Pie
Ho - ney Pie
Ho - ney Pie
(Free)
I love you
Ho-ney Pie

WITH A LITTLE HELP FROM MY FRIENDS

Words & Music by John Lennon & Paul McCartney.

A
E
B
F♯m7
B7
E
E
B
What would you think if I sang out of tune would you stand up and walk out on me
Lend me your ears and I'll sing
F♯m7
B7
E
B
D
A
E
you a song and I'll try not to sing out of key
oh I get by with a lit-tle help from my friends
Mm, I get high
4
4
T
A
B

D
A
E
A
E
B
with a lit-tle help from my friends
Mm, gon-na try with a lit-tle help from my friends
C
E
B
F#m7
B7
E
What do I do when my love is a-way does it wor - ry you to be a-lone ?

E
B
F#m7
B7
E
How do I feel by the end of the day are you sad be-cause you're on your own No I get by
4
4
T
A
B
D
D
A
E
D
A
with a lit-tle help from my friends Mm, I get high with a lit-tle help from my friends
D.S.X (Mm, gon-na try with a lit-tle help from my friends

E
A
to ⊕ E
E C#m
Mm, gon-na try with a lit-tle help from my friends Do you need a-ny-bo-
Oh I get high)
F#
E
D
A
C#m
F#
-dy? I need some-bo-dy to love
I just need some-one to love
Could it be a-ny-bo-dy? I

E
D
1.
A
F
E
B
F#m7
want some - bo - dy to love
Would you be - lieve in a love at first sight yes I'm cer -
B7
E
E
B
F#m7
- tain that it hap - pens all the time
What do you see when you turn out the light? I can't tell

F#m7
B7
E
2.
A
Coda
E
— you but I know — it's mine — oh — I get by — — oh, — I get by —
— Yes — I get by
D.S.
D
A
C
D
E
— with a lit-tle help — from my friends — with a lit-tle help — from my friends
(Ah)

WITHIN YOU WITHOUT YOU

Words & Music by George Harrison.

In Tempo
Fill in
2x only
A
We were talk - ing a - bout the
talk - ing a - bout the
talk - ing a - bout the

space be - tween us all and the peo - ple who
love we all could share When we find it to
love that's gone so cold and the peo - ple who
hide them - selves be - hind a wall of il - lu - sion
try our best to hold it there with our
gain the world and lose their soul They don't
to
1.
2x only
T A B

ne - ver glimpse the truth, then it's far too late when they pass a -
- way
We were love, with our
2.

love we could save the world if they on - ly knew
a tempo
B
Try to re - al -
And to see you're
1x tacet
TAB
TAB

1.
- ize it's all with in your - self, no one else can make you change
rea - ly on - ly ver - y small and
2.
life flows on with - in you, and with - out you
C a tempo
T
A
B

(Pizz)

T
A
B
Tempo Rubato

In Tempo
We were
Coda
know
they can't
D.S.

see
Are you one of them
T
A
B
T
A
B
T
A
B
T
A
B

D
1.
When you've seen be - yond your - self then you may find, peace of mind, is wait - ing there
And the time will come when you see we're all one, and
2x
2.
life flows on with - in you and with - out you

THE WORD

Words & Music by John Lennon & Paul McCartney.

D7(#9)
G7
D7(#9)
word and be like me Say the word I'm think-ing of Have you heard the word is
word and be like me Spread the word I'm think-ing of Have you heard the word is
word is just the way It's the word I'm think-ing of And the on - ly word is
word is just the way It's the word I'm think-ing of And the on - ly word is
Asus4 A Gsus4 A D7(#9)
to ⊕
love ? love ? love
It's so fine, It's sun - shine It's the word lo - ve
love
T.C.
H.H.

B
D7
Cadd9
F6
1.2.
G7
In the begin-ning I mis-un-der-stood But now I've got it, the wo-rd is good Spread the
Everywhere I go I hear it said In the good and the bad books that I have read Say the
Now that I know what I feel must be right I'm here to show every
3.
G7
bo-dy the light Give the
Coda
D7(#9)
lo-ve
C
D7
Cadd9
(Organ)
Give the
D.S.

F6
G7
D7(#9)
D
D7(#9)
Say the word
(Chorus)
Say the word
lo - ve
Say the word
G7
lo - ve
Say the word
D7(#9)
lo - ve
Say the word
lo - ve
Say the word

D7(#9)
Asus4
A
Gsus4
G
D7(#9)
Lo - ve
Say the word
lo - ve
Lo - ve
Say the word
Lo - ve
T.C.
T.C.
E
D7
Cadd9
F6
G7
(Organ)
Fade Out

WORDS OF LOVE

Words & Music by Buddy Holly.

D E A D E A
tell me how you feel
whis - per soft and true
the words I long to hear
Tell me love is real
Dar - ling I love you
Dar - ling when you're near
D E A D E to⊕ B A D E
um um um um
2x
A D E A D E A

D E C A D E A D E
A D E A D E
Coda
A
um
D E A D E A D E
um um Ah Ah Ah
D.S.
Repeat & Fade Out

YELLOW SUBMARINE

Words & Music by John Lennon & Paul McCartney.

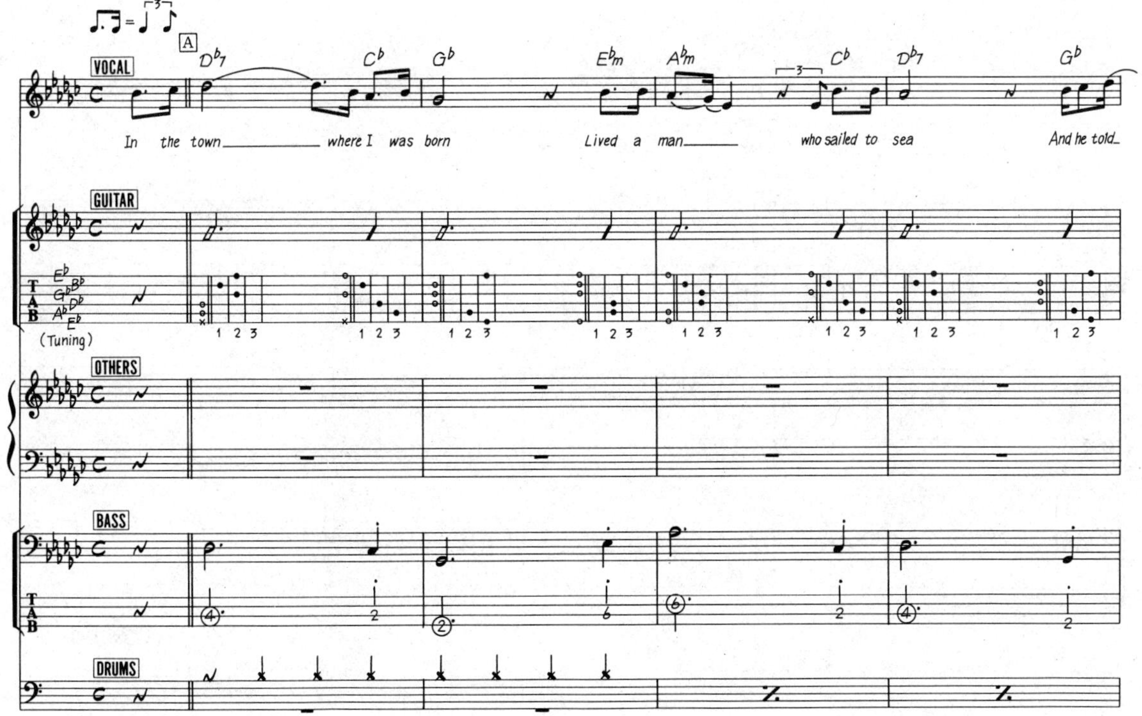

D♭7
C♭
G♭
E♭m
A♭m
C♭
D♭7
G♭
us of his life
In the land
of sub - ma - rines
So we
4.
B
D♭7
C♭
G♭
E♭m
A♭m
C♭
D♭7
G♭
sailed
up to the sun
Till we found
a sea of green
And we
live
a life of ease
Eve - ry one of us
has all we need
Sky of

D♭7
C♭
G♭
E♭m
A♭m
C♭
D♭7
lived ____ be-neath the waves In our yellow ___ sub - ma-rine
blue ____ and sea of green In our yellow ___ sub - ma-rine
T
A
B
1 2 3

C
G♭
D♭7
G♭
We all live in a yel - low sub - ma-rine
Yel - low sub - ma-rine
Yel - low sub - ma-rine
T
A
B
1 2 3

to Φ
1.
G♭
D♭7
G♭
We all live in a yel - low sub - ma-rine
Yel - low sub - ma-rine
Yel - low sub - ma-rine
And our friends
D
D♭7
C♭
G♭
E♭m
A♭m
C♭
D♭7
G♭
are all a - board
Ma - ny more of them
live next door
And the

D♭7
C♭
G♭
D♭7
G♭
D♭7
D♭7
G♭
band ___ be-gins to ___ play ___
(Brass)
2.
G♭
E
D♭7
C♭
G♭
E♭m
A♭m
C♭
yel - low sub - ma-rine
(Full speed ahead Mr. Boatswain, full speed

D♭7
G♭
C♭
E♭m
A♭m
ahead. Full speed ahead it is, Sgt.
Cut the cable, drop the cable
Aye, Sir, aye
Captain, Captain) As we
D.S.

Coda
F
G♭
D♭7
yel - low sub-ma-rine
We all live in a yel - low sub-ma-rine
Yel - low sub-ma-rine
yel - low sub-ma-rine
Repeat & Fade Out

YER BLUES

Words & Music by John Lennon & Paul McCartney.

E
G
B7
to
1.
E A E/B B7
die
If I
ain't dead al-ready
Ooh
girl you know the rea-son
why
In the mor-
die
If I
ain't dead al-ready
Ooh
girl you know the rea-son
2.
E A E/B B7
B
(3 times Repeat)
why
My
mo-ther was of the sky
My fa-ther was of the earth
But I am of the u-ni-verse
And
ea - gle picks my eye
The worm he licks my bone
I feel so su-i-ci-dal
Just like
Black cloud crossed my mind
Blue mist round my soul
Feel so su-i-ci-dal
E-ven

1. 2.
E
A
E
G
you know what it's worth
Dy - lan's Mis-ter Jones
I'm lo - ne - ly
Lone - ly
wan - na die
wan - na die
If I ain't dead al - rea - dy
If I ain't dead al - rea - dy
B7
E
A
E/B
B7
3.
E7
A
C
Ooh girl you know the rea - son why
Ooh girl you know the rea - son why
The hate my rock and roll wanna die

A
E
G
yeah___ wan-na die______
If I ain't dead al - rea-dy Ooh
B7
E
A
E
B
B7
D
E
girl_____ you know the rea-son why
(Dubbing Snare)

E
A
T
A
B
E
G
B7

E
A
E/B
B7
E
E
A
8va

E
G
B7
N.C.
Yes I'm
D.S.
Coda
E
A
E/B
B7
why
Yes I'm lone - ly
wan - na die
Yes I'm
Fade Out

YES IT IS

Words & Music by John Lennon & Paul McCartney.

D B7 C#m E/B A D
1. C#m E
- night. For red is the col-or that my ba-by wore___ and what's more___ it's true, Yes it___ is.
sure. I would re-mem-ber all the things we planned,___ un-der-stand___ it's
2. C#m E E7
B Bm E
true, Yes it is, it's true, Yes it___ is. I could be hap-py___ with

A
F#m
Bm
E
C#m
C#m7/E
F#
B7
Ah
you by my side, If I could for-get her but it's my pride, Yes it is, Yes it is, Oh, Yes it is. Yeh.
C
E
A
F#m7
B7
D
Please don't wear red to-night, This is what I said to-night. For
8va
Harm.
Harm

C#m
E/G#
A
D
to Coda
C#m
E
E7
red is the col-or that will make me blue__ in spite of you__ it's true. Yes it is, it's true, Yes it__ is.
T
A
B
D.S.
Coda
C#m
E
G#7
A
B7
E
true, Yes it is, it's true, Yes it is, it's true.

YESTERDAY

Words & Music by John Lennon & Paul McCartney.

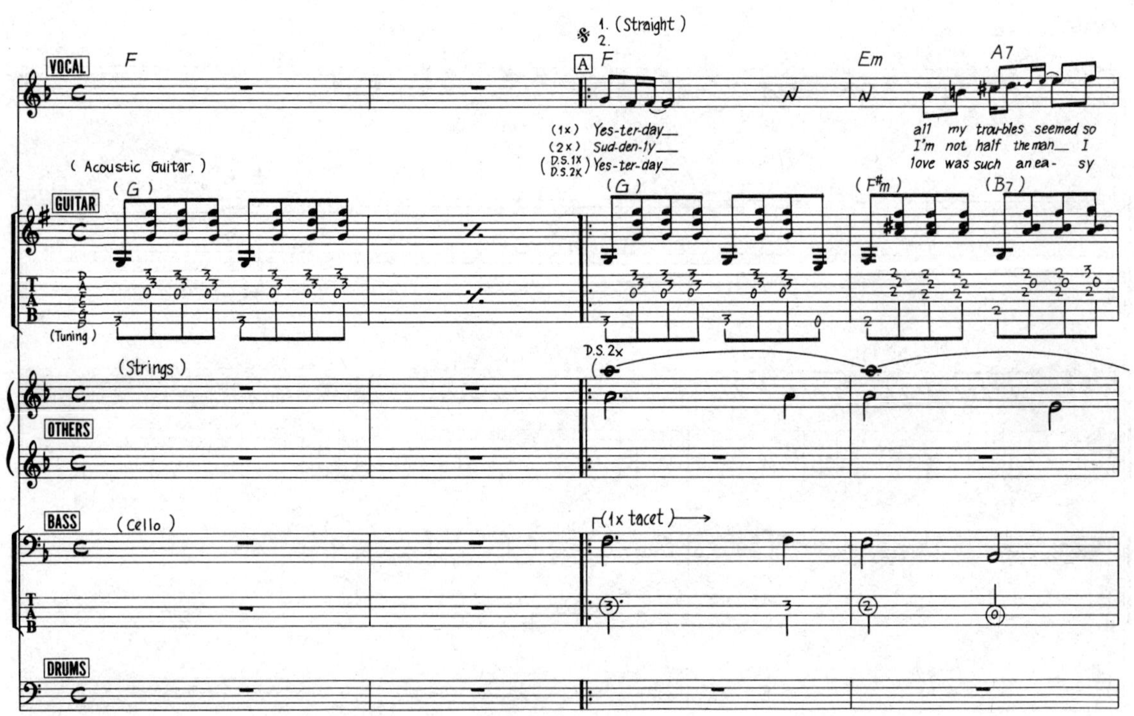

Dm
Dm7/C
B♭
C7
F
F/E
far a - way
used to be
game to play
Now it looks as through they're here to stay Oh
There's a sha - dow hang - ing o - ver me Oh
Now I need a place to hide a - way Oh
(Em)
(Em7/D)
(C)
(D7)
(G)
(G/F♯)

Dm7
G7
B♭
F
B
A7sus4
A7
Dm
C
B♭
Dm/A
I be - lieve in yes - ter - day
Yes - ter - day came sud - den - ly
I be - lieve in yes - ter - day
Why she had to go I don't
(Em7)
(A7)
(C)
(G)
2x
(B7 sus4)
(B7)
(Em)
(D)
(C)
(Em/B)

Gm6
C7
F
Asus4
A7
Dm
C
B♭
Dm/A
know she would - n't say
I said some - thing wrong now I
(Am6)
(D7)
(G)
(B7 sus4)
(B7)
(Em)
(D)
(C)
(Em/B)
D.S.1×
long for yes - ter - day
DS.1(- day)
Coda
G7
rit.
Mm
(A7)
D.S.1.
2. al Coda

YOU CAN'T DO THAT

Words & Music by John Lennon & Paul McCartney.

G7
C7
cause you pain___ If I catch you talk-ing to that boy a - gain I'm gon-na let you down___
- ing to him___ Do I have to tell you one more time I think it's a sin I think I'll let you down___
Chorus
let you down___
G7
gon-na let you down and leave you___ flat___
D7
and leave you flat___
and leave you flat___
Be-cause I told you be-fore___ oh___
Be-cause I told you be-fore___ oh___

C7
G7
1.
D7
2.
B
B7
You can't do that
You can't do that
Well it's the
Ev'-ry-bo-dy's green
Em
Am
Bm
G7
B7
Em
'Cause I'm the one who won your love
But if they'd seen
you
D.S.x

C
Am
Bm
D7
G7
talk-ing that way
they'd laugh in my face
So
please lis-ten to me if you wan-na stay mine
I can't help my feel-ing I'll go
D.S.x
1 2 3
2 3 4
1 2 3
3 4 5 6
C7
Chorus
let you down
gon-na let you down and leave you flat
out of my mind you know I'll let you down
And leave you flat
Be-cause I've
H

D7
C7
G7
D7
D G7
Chorus
You
told you be-fore
oh
You can't do
that
wah
can't do that
You can't do that
C7
You can't do that
h.c
C
D

G7
you can't do that
D7
C7
you can't do that
G7
Ev'-ry-bo-dy's green
Coda
G
rit.
that
D.S.

YOU KNOW MY NAME (LOOK UP THE NUMBER)

Words & Music by John Lennon & Paul McCartney.

G
A7
A
G
$G^{b}7aug$
B^{b}
Bm7
E7(9)
You know my name
Look up the num-ber
G
D
Em7
A7
D
F#m7
G
A7
You know my name
Look up the num-ber
You
you know
you know my name

D
F#m7
G
A7
D
B Faster with a latin beat
you
you know
you know my name
D
A7
D
(Spoken); Good evening and welcome to slaggers featuring Denis O'Bell
Come on Ringo
Let's hear it for Denis

A7
C
G
(3 times)
F#aug
Bm7
E7
Good evening
(1x) You know my name
(2x) You know my name Ba ba ba ba ba ba ba ba ba
(3x) You know my name Ba ba ba ba
Bet-ter look up my num-ber
look up my num-ber
look up the num-ber
G
D
Em
A7
D
A7
You know my name That's right Look up my num-ber You you know you know my name
You know my name That's right Look up the num-ber Oh wu You know you know you know my name
You know my name Look up the num-ber You You know you know my name ba-by
2x

D
A7
D
A7
D
You you know___ you know my name___
You know you know you know my name
You know you know you know my name___
You know you know my name___ you know you know my
A7
name
(Spoken) Go on Denis let's hear it for Denis O'Bell
You know my name
D
D F#
G
A7
D
D F#
You know my name
You
you know my
num-ber
you know my
You know you know you know my name you know you know
(Cuckow)

G A7 G D/F# Bm E7
name you know my num-ber
you know my name Prrr prrr you know my name and the num-ber You know my name Look up the num-
G D Em A7 E D D/F# G A7
You know my num - ber Look up the num-ber You know my name you know my num-ber two you
-ber you know you know my name Yes you know my name you know you know my
T
A
B

D
D/F#
G
A7
D
D/F#
G
G#dim
A7
know my num-ber three you know my num-ber four oh
You know my name you know my num-ber too
You know my name you know my num-ber
name you know my name
Look up my num-ber you know
D6
What's up with you? Ha!
You know my name
That's right
Yeah
(with Brush)

F
D
F#m7
G
A7sus4
D
F#m7
Gadd9
A7sus4
G6
(ad lib. voice)
T
A
B
1 2 3
2 3 4
3 4 5
1 2 3
Gb7aug/Bb
Bm7
E7(9)
G
D
Em7

A7
G
D
F#m7
G
A7
D
F#m7
G
A7
(Tenor Sax)
D
F#m7
G
G#dim
A7
D13
tr.

YOU LIKE ME TOO MUCH

Words & Music by George Harrison.

Am
C
G
Am
- ning you'll be back a - gain to night tell- ing me there'll be no next time if I just
me but you have - n't got the nerve to walk out and make me lone - ly which is all
C
G
Bm7
D7
don't treat you right You'll ne- ver leave me and you know it's true
that I de - serve You'll ne- ver leave me and you know it's true

(Straight)
D7
B G
C
D7
1.
'Cause you like me too much and I like you
You've
(Electric. Piano)
2.
C G/F
G/B
Em7
A7
Bm
I really do
And it's nice when you be-lieve
D.S.×
(Tambourine)

A
Em7
A7
A7
D7
D
Am
me
If you
leave me
I will fol-low you and bring you back
C
G
Am
C
where you be-long
'Cause I could-n't real-ly stand it
I ad-mit that I was wrong
D.S.×('Cause I could-n't)
D.S.×
4
4.

G
Bm7
D7
I would-n't let you leave me 'cause it's true 'cause you
G
C
D7
to
E G
like me too much and I like you
(Acoustic Piano)
(Tambourine)

G
C
G
tr.
D7
'Cause you
D.S.

Coda
D7
F
G
C
D7
'Cause you like me too much and I like you
(Acoustic Piano)
T
A
B
1 2 3
G
Bb
D7
G
tr.
(Tambourine)

YOU NEVER GIVE ME YOUR MONEY

Words & Music by John Lennon & Paul McCartney.

Bm7-5
E7
Am
A
Am7
(Upper Part 1x Tacet)
Dm7
You nev- er give me your mo - ney
I nev- er give you my num - ber
1x only
2x only
1 x Tacet
G7
C
FΔ7
1.
You on- ly give me your fun - ny pa- per And in the mid- dle of ne - go - ti - a - tions you break down
I on- ly give you my sit - u - a - tion And in the mid- dle of in - ves - ti - ga - tion I

2.
B
Am
C
G
G7
C
E7
break down
Out of col-lege mo-ney spent
8va
H.H
F
See no fu-ture pay no rent
All the mo-ney's gone no-where to go
A-ny job-ber got the sack

Am
C7
F
G7
C
C
B♭
F
Mon-day morn-ing turn-ing back
Yel-low lor-ry slow
no-where to go.
But oh
that ma-gic feel-ing
no-where to
8va bassa
Cym.
C
B♭
F
C
go
Oh
that ma-gic feel-ing
no-- where to go
no-where to go

D
B♭
F
C
Ah
Ooo
(E.G.) Piano Simile ~
cym. ~

E
C
D7
E♭7
G7
C7
A7
E♭7
C7
F♯
E♭
F
A
One sweet dream
cym.
H.H.

B
C
E
A
Dm
G/D
Pick up the bags and get in the lim-ou-sine
Soon we'll be a-way from here
Am/D
G/D
A
B
G
C
G/B
Step on the gas and wipe that tear a-way
One sweet dream, came true to-day

A
C
G
B
came true
to-day
x x x x x x
One, two, three, four, five, six, se-ven, All good child-ren go to hea-ven.
H.H
(Ad lib.)
2 x only
Q.C
Repeat & Fade Out

YOU'RE GOING TO LOSE THAT GIRL

Words & Music by John Lennon & Paul McCartney.

𝄋 (Straight)
B E
G#m
F#m
(1X, D.S.x) She's going to
(2X) You're going to
B7
change her mind
find her gone
(1X, D.S.x) If you don't take her out to-night she's going to change her mind
(2X) If you don't treat her right my friend You're going to find her gone
2x
2x. D.S.x
2x. D.S.x
2x.D.S.x
E
G#m
F#m
I'm going to
You're not the
B7
treat her kind
on - ly one
And I will take her out to-night And I will treat her kind
'Cause I will treat her right and then You'll be the lone - ly one
You're going to
You're going to
2x. D.S.x
2x D.S.x

C E
C#m
F#m
B7
Yes Yes You're going to lose that girl
Yes Yes You're going to lose that girl
lose that girl
You're going to lose that girl
You're going to
2x S
F#m
Yes Yes You're going to
to
D
lose that girl
lose
D
G
C
I'll make a point of tak-ing her a-way from you
D.S.x
2x

G
What would you do
Yeah!
C
The way you treat her
what else can I do
2x
1 2 3
x
1.
F
E
E
G#m
F#m
You're going to
4 5 6
2 3 4

B7
lose that girl
E
G#m
F#m
You're going to
4
D
C
S
2.
F
You're going to
Coda
D
A
E
lose
that
girl
that
girl
D.S.

YOUR MOTHER SHOULD KNOW

Words & Music by John Lennon & Paul McCartney.

A7/E
2x D.S.1x (A7)
Dm
G7
C
C/B
A7
hit be-fore your mo ther was born
hit be fore your mo ther was born
da da da da da da da da
Though she was born a long long time a-go your mo-ther should know
2x. D.S.1x
D7
G7
C
E7
D.S. 1x, 2x
to ⊕ 1. 2.
1.
Your mo-ther should know
Sing it a-gain
D.S.1X, D.S.2X (Ooo Ooo)
2x. D.S.2x
Your mo-ther should
(1x) Ah
(2x, D.S.1x) Ah
(D.S.2x) Yeah
1 x tacet

B
2.
E
Am
F△7
F△7/G
(Organ)
Ah
C
E7
(Organ)
Coda 1
A7
D7
Your mo - ther should know
Ah
Your
H P
D.S. 1

G7
C
C
E
Am
Your mo-ther should know
(Organ)
mo- ther should
Ah
Ah
F∆7
F∆7
G
C
E7
Sing it a-gain
D.S. 2

Coda 2.
A7
D7
G7
C
Your mo-ther should know
your mo-ther should know
(Organ)
Ah
Your
mo - ther
should
Yeah
A7
D7
G7
C
your mo-ther should
your mo ther should know
Ah
Your
mo - ther
should
Yeah

YOU'VE GOT TO HIDE YOUR LOVE AWAY

Words & Music by John Lennon & Paul McCartney.

C F C
D
B
G D F G C F C
Feel-ing two foot small
In the state I'm in
Ev'-ry-where peo-ple stare each and ev'ry-day
How could she say to me "Love will find a way?"
(Tambourine 1x in)
G D F G C F C D D/C D/B D/A
C
G C
I can see them laugh at me And I hear them say
Gath-er round all you clowns Let me hear you say
Hey you've got to hide your love a-
(Arpeggio)
(Shaker)

Dsus4 D Dadd9 D
G C
Dsus4 D Dadd9 D
D G D F G
(Flute)
- way
Hey you've got to hide your love a - way
C F C G D F G C F C G

YOU'VE REALLY GOT A HOLD ON ME

Words & Music by William Robinson.

𝄋 (Straight)
A
A
G#m F#m
E
I don't like you, but I love you See that I'm al - way - s thinking of you
I don't want you, but I need you Don't want to kiss you but I need you
I want to leave you, don't want to stay here Don't want to spend a - no - ther day here
2X D.S.x
A A7 D B7 E7 A
Oh, oh, oh, you treat me bad - ly I love you mad - ly
Oh, oh, oh, you do me wrong now, my love is strong Now
Oh, oh, oh, I want to split now I just can quit now
You've real - ly got a hold on me
(Chorus)
You've real - ly got a

A
G#m
F#m
E
B
A
A7
You've real-ly got a hold on me
2x(hold on me)
ba - by I love you and all I
hold on me
You've real-ly got a hold on me
D
A
E7
to C
A
A/F#
want you to do Is just to hold me, hold me, hold me, hold me
D.S.(please squeeze)
(Aco. Piano)
D.S.(you've)

F#m E A A A/F# F#m E A
ti-red ti-red
Coda D
A
real-ly got a hold on me
Chorus
you've
D.S.
G#m F#m E A
you've real-ly got a hold on me
real-ly got a hold on me
you've real-ly got a hold on me

YOU WON'T SEE ME

Words & Music by John Lennon & Paul McCartney.

D
A
B7
D
- ne's en-gaged
I have had
e-nough
So a -
- ct your age
- nt to hide
But I can't
get through
My ha -
- nds are tied
woo
la la la
woo
la la la
woo
4
A
A7
D
Dm
We have lost
the time
that was so
hard
to find
I won't want
to stay
I don't have
much
to say
la la la
woo
la la la
woo

A
B7
D
A
And_ I will lose
But_ I can't turn
my mind___
a-way___
If
And
you won't see me___
la la la
woo___
la la la
you won't see me
T
A
B
9 10 11
11 12 13
10 11 12
9 10 11
(T.C.)
(Tambourine)
(H.H.)
D
A
1.
2.
B
Bm
you won't see me___
I don't know___
Time af-ter time_
you won't see me
you won't see me
7 8 9
(T.C)
(Tambourine)
(H.H.)
(H.H.)

Dm
Ddim
A
B7
You re - fuse to e-ven lis - ten
I would-n't mind If I knew
D/E
E7
C A
B7
D
what I was miss - ing
Though the days are few
They're fill - ed with tears
know what I was know what I was woo
la la la woo
2x
2x

A
B7
D
A
And since I
lost you
It fee - ls like years
Yes, it seems
la la la
woo
la la la
woo
la la la
4.
A7
D
Dm
A
so long
Girl, since you've been gone
And I just can't go on
woo
la la la
woo
la la la
woo

B7
D
D A
to Coda
If you won't see me
you won't see me
la la la
you won't see me
you won't see me
(T.C.)
(Tambourine)
(H.H.)
D.S.
Coda
D A
B7
D
A
you won't see me
woo
la la la
woo
la la la
Repeat & Fade Out

THE BEATLES BRITISH SINGLES

MY BONNIE/THE SAINTS
(both sides by Tony Sheridan and The Beatles)
(Polydor NH 66-833) January 1962

LOVE ME DO/P.S. I LOVE YOU
(Parlophone R 4949) October, 1962

PLEASE PLEASE ME/ASK ME WHY
Parlophone R4983 January 1963

FROM ME TO YOU/THANK YOU GIRL
(Parlophone R 5015) April 1963

SHE LOVES YOU/I'LL GET YOU
(Parlophone R 5055) August 1963

I WANT TO HOLD YOUR HAND/THIS BOY
(Parlophone R 5084) November 1963

SWEET GEORGIA BROWN/NOBODY'S CHILD
(both sides with Tony Sheridan)
(Polydor NH 52-906) January 1964

WHY/CRY FOR A SHADOW
(A-side with Tony Sheridan)
(Polydor NH 52-275) February 1964

CAN'T BUY ME LOVE/YOU CAN'T DO THAT
(Parlophone R 5114) March 1964

AIN'T SHE SWEET/IF YOU LOVE ME BABY
(B-side with Tony Sheridan)
(Polydor NH 52-317) May 1964

A HARD DAY'S NIGHT/THINGS WE SAID TODAY
(Parlophone R 5160) July 1964

I FEEL FINE/SHE'S A WOMAN
(Parlophone R 5200) November 1964

TICKET TO RIDE/YES IT IS
(Parlophone R 5265) April 1965

HELP!/I'M DOWN
(Parlophone R 5305) July 1965

DAY TRIPPER/WE CAN WORK IT OUT
(Parlophone R 5389) December 1965

PAPERBACK WRITER/RAIN
(Parlophone R 5452) June 1966

YELLOW SUBMARINE/ELEANOR RIGBY
(Parlophone R 5493) August 1966

PENNY LANE/STRAWBERRY FIELDS FOREVER
(Parlophone R 5570) February 1967

ALL YOU NEED IS LOVE/BABY YOU'RE A RICH MAN
(Parlophone R 5620) July 1967

HELLO GOODBYE/I AM THE WALRUS
(Parlophone R5655) November 1967

LADY MADONNA/THE INNER LIGHT
(Parlophone R5675) March 1968

HEY JUDE/REVOLUTION
(Apple R 5722) August 1968

GET BACK/DON'T LET ME DOWN
(Apple R 5777) April 1969

THE BALLAD OF JOHN AND YOKO/OLD BROWN SHOE
(Apple R 5786) May 1969

SOMETHING/COME TOGETHER
(Apple R 5814) October 1969

LET IT BE/YOU KNOW MY NAME (LOOK UP THE NUMBER)
(Apple R 5833) March 1970

TWIST AND SHOUT (LIVE)/FALLING IN LOVE AGAIN (LIVE)
(Lingasong NB1) June 1977

SEARCHIN'/MONEY/TILL THERE WAS YOU
(Audiofidelity AFS 1) October 1982

THE BEATLES BRITISH ALBUMS

PLEASE PLEASE ME

I Saw Her Standing There/Misery/Anna/Chains/Boys/Ask Me Why/Please Please Me/Love Me Do/P.S. I Love You/Baby It's You/Do You Want To Know A Secret/A Taste Of Honey/There's A Place/Twist And Shout
(Parlophone PMC 1202, mono; PCS 3042, stereo) March 1963

WITH THE BEATLES

It Won't Be Long/All I've Got To Do/All My Loving/Don't Bother Me/Little Child/Till There Was You/Please Mr Postman/Roll Over Beethoven/Hold Me Tight/You Really Got A Hold On Me/I Wanna Be Your Man/Devil In Her Heart/Not A Second Time/Money
(Parlophone PMC 1206, mono; PCS 3045, stereo)
November 1963

THE BEATLES' FIRST

(with Tony Sheridan)
Ain't She Sweet/Cry For A Shadow/My Bonnie/If You Love Me Baby/Sweet Georgia Brown/The Saints/Why/Nobody's Child
(plus 4 tracks not by The Beatles)
(Polydor 236 201) June 1964

LONG TALL SALLY

(7 inch E.P.)
Long Tall Sally/I Call Your Name/Slow Down/Matchbox
(Parlophone GEP 8913) June 1964

A HARD DAY'S NIGHT

A Hard Day's Night/I Should Have Known Better/If I Fell/I'm Happy Just To Dance With You/And I Love Her/Tell Me Why/Can't Buy Me Love/Any Time At All/I'll Cry Instead/Things We Said Today
When I Get Home/You Can't Do That/I'll Be Back
(Parlophone PMC 1230, mono, PCS 3058, stereo) July 1964

BEATLES FOR SALE

No Reply/I'm A Loser/Baby's In Black/Rock And Roll Music/I'll Follow The Sun/Mr Moonlight/Kansas City: Hey Hey Hey Hey/Eight Days A Week/Words Of Love/Honey Don't/Every Little Thing/I Don't Want To Spoil The Party/What You're Doing/Everybody's Trying To Be My Baby
(Parlophone PMC 1240, mono; PCS 3062, stereo)
December 1964

HELP!

Help!/The Night Before/You've Got To Hide Your Love Away
I Need You/Another Girl/You're Gonna Lose That Girl
Ticket To Ride/Act Naturally/It's Only Love/You Like Me Too Much
Tell Me What You See/Yesterday/Dizzy Miss Lizzy
(Parlophone PMC 1255, mono; PCS 3071, stereo)
August 1965

RUBBER SOUL

Drive My Car/Norwegian Wood/You Won't See Me/Nowhere Man/Think For Yourself/The Word/Michelle/What Goes On/Girl/I'm Looking Through You/In My Life/Wait/If I Needed Someone/Run For Your Life
(Parlophone PMC 1267, mono; PCS 3075, stereo)
December 1965

REVOLVER

Taxman/Eleanor Rigby/I'm Only Sleeping/Love You To/Here There And Everywhere/Yellow Submarine/She Said She Said/Good Day Sunshine
And Your Bird Can Sing/For No One/Dr Robert/I Want To Tell You
Got To Get You Into My Life/Tomorrow Never Knows
(Parlophone PMC 7009, mono; PCS 7009, stereo)
August 1966

A COLLECTION OF BEATLES OLDIES

She Loves You/From Me To You/We Can Work It Out/Help!/Michelle/Yesterday/I Feel Fine/Yellow Submarine/Can't Buy Me Love/Bad Boy/Day Tripper/A Hard Day's Night/Ticket To Ride/Paperback Writer/Eleanor Rigby/I Want To Hold Your Hand
(Parlophone PMC 7016, mono; PCS 7016, stereo)
December 1966

SGT. PEPPER'S LONELY HEARTS CLUB BAND

Sgt. Pepper's Lonely Hearts Club Band/With A Little Help From My Friends/Lucy In The Sky With Diamonds/It's Getting Better/Fixing A Hole/She's Leaving Home/Being For The Benefit Of Mr Kite/Within You Without You/When I'm 64/Lovely Rita/Good Morning Good Morning/Sgt. Pepper's Lonely Hearts Club Band (reprise)
A Day In The Life
(Parlophone PMC 7027, mono; PCS 7027, stereo)
June 1967

MAGICAL MYSTERY TOUR

(double 7 inch EP set)
Magical Mystery Tour/Your Mother Should Know/I Am The Walrus
Fool On The Hill/Flying/Blue Jay Way
(Parlophone MMT1, mono; SMMT1, stereo) December 1967

THE BEATLES

(double album)
Back In The USSR/Dear Prudence/Glass Onion/Ob-La-Di,Ob-La-Da
Wild Honey Pie/The Continuing Story Of Bungalow Bill/While My Guitar Gently Weeps/Happiness Is A Warm Gun/Martha My Dear/I'm So Tired/Blackbird/Piggies/Rocky Raccoon/Don't Pass Me By/Why Don't We Do It In The Road/I Will/Julia/Birthday/Yer Blues/Mother Nature's Son/Everybody's Got Something To Hide Except For Me And My Monkey/Sexy Sadie/Helter Skelter/Long Long Long/ Revolution 1
Honey Pie/Savoy Truffle/Cry Baby Cry/Revolution 9/Goodnight
(Apple PMC 7067/8, mono; PCS 7067/8, stereo)
November 1968

YELLOW SUBMARINE

Yellow Submarine/Only A Northern Song/All Together Now
Hey Bulldog/It's All Too Much/All You Need Is Love
(plus six tracks by George Martin and his Orchestra)
(Apple PMC 7070, mono; PCS 7070, stereo) January 1969

ABBEY ROAD

Come Together/Something/Maxwell's Silver Hammer
Oh! Darling/Octopus's Garden/I Want You (She's So Heavy)/Here Comes The Sun/Because/You Never Give Me Your Money/Sun King/Mean Mr Mustard/Polythene Pam/She Came In Through The Bathroom Window/Golden Slumbers/Carry That Weight/The End/Her Majesty
(Apple PCS 7088) September 1969

LET IT BE

(boxed album with book)
Two Of Us/Dig A Pony/Across The Universe/I Me Mine/Dig It
Let It Be/Maggie Mae/I've Got A Feeling/The One After 909/The Long
And Winding Road/For You Blue/Get Back
(Apple PXS 1) May 1970

THE BEATLES AT THE HOLLYWOOD BOWL

Twist And Shout/She's A Woman/Dizzy Miss Lizzy/Ticket To Ride
Can't Buy Me Love/Things We Said Today/Roll Over Beethoven/Boys
A Hard Day's Night/Help!/All My Loving/She Loves You/Long Tall Sally
(EMI EMTV 4) May 1977

THE BEATLES LIVE AT THE STAR CLUB, HAMBURG, GERMANY, 1962

(double album)
I Saw Her Standing There/Roll Over Beethoven/Hippy Hippy Shake
Sweet Little Sixteen/Lend Me Your Comb/Your Feet's Too Big
Twist And Shout/Mr Moonlight/A Taste Of Honey/Besame
Mucho/Reminiscing/Kansas City:Hey Hey Hey Hey/Nothin' Shakin'
To Know Her Is To Love Her/Little Queenie/Falling In Love Again
Ask Me Why/Be-Bop-A-Lula/Hallelujah I Love Her So/Red Sails In The
Sunset/Everybody's Trying To Be My Baby/Matchbox/I'm Talkin' Bout
You/I Wish I Could Shimmy Like My Sister Kate/Long Tall Sally
I Remember You
(Lingasong LNL 1) May 1977

THE COMPLETE SILVER BEATLES

Three Cool Cats/Crying Waiting Hoping/Besame Mucho/Searchin'
The Sheik Of Araby/Money/To Know Her Is To Love Her/Take Good Care
Of My Baby/Memphis Tennessee/Sure To Fall/Till There Was
You/September In The Rain
(Audiofidelity AFELP 1047) September 1982

THE BEATLES AMERICAN SINGLES

MY BONNIE/THE SAINTS

(with Tony Sheridan)
(Decca 31382) April 1962

PLEASE PLEASE ME/ASK ME WHY

(Vee Jay VJ 498) February 1963

FROM ME TO YOU/THANK YOU GIRL

(Vee Jay VJ 522) May 1963

SHE LOVES YOU/I'LL GET YOU

(Swan 4152) September 1963

I WANT TO HOLD YOUR HAND/I SAW HER STANDING THERE

(Capitol 5112) January 1964

MY BONNIE/THE SAINTS

(with Tony Sheridan)
(MGM K 13213) January 1964

PLEASE PLEASE ME/FROM ME TO YOU

(Vee Jay VJ 581) January 1964

TWIST AND SHOUT/THERE'S A PLACE

(Tollie 9001) March 1964

CAN'T BUY ME LOVE/YOU CAN'T DO THAT

(Capitol 5150) March 1964

DO YOU WANT TO KNOW A SECRET/THANK YOU GIRL

(Vee Jay VJ 587) March 1964

WHY/CRY FOR A SHADOW

(A-side with Tony Sheridan)
(MGM K 13227) March 1964

LOVE ME DO/ P.S. I LOVE YOU

(Tollie 9008) April 1964

SIE LIEBT DICH/I'LL GET YOU

(Swan 4182) May 1964

SWEET GEORGIA BROWN/IF YOU LOVE ME BABY
(with Tony Sheridan)
(Atco 6302) June 1964

AIN'T SHE SWEET/NOBODY'S CHILD
(B-side with Tony Sheridan)
(Atco 6308) July 1964

A HARD DAY'S NIGHT/I SHOULD HAVE KNOWN BETTER
(Capitol 5222) July 1964

I'LL CRY INSTEAD/I'M HAPPY JUST TO DANCE WITH YOU
(Capitol 5234) July 1964

AND I LOVE HER/IF I FELL
(Capitol 5235) July 1964

SLOW DOWN/MATCHBOX
(Capitol 5255) August 1964

I FEEL FINE/SHE'S A WOMAN
(Capitol 5327) November 1964

EIGHT DAYS A WEEK/I DON'T WANT TO SPOIL THE PARTY
(Capitol 5371) February 1965

TICKET TO RIDE/YES IT IS
(Capitol 5407) April 1965

HELP!/I'M DOWN
(Capitol 5476) July 1965

YESTERDAY/ACT NATURALLY
(Capitol 5498) September 1965

DAY TRIPPER/WE CAN WORK IT OUT
(Capitol 5555) December 1965

NOWHERE MAN/WHAT GOES ON
(Capitol 5587) February 1966

PAPERBACK WRITER/RAIN
(Capitol 5651) May 1966

YELLOW SUBMARINE/ELEANOR RIGBY
(Capitol 5715) August 1966

PENNY LANE/STRAWBERRY FIELDS FOREVER
(Capitol 5810) February 1967

ALL YOU NEED IS LOVE/BABY YOU'RE A RICH MAN
(Capitol 5964) July 1967

HELLO GOODBYE/I AM THE WALRUS
(Capitol 2056) November 1967

LADY MADONNA/THE INNER LIGHT
(Capitol 2138) March 1968

HEY JUDE/REVOLUTION
(Apple 2276) August 1968

GET BACK/DON'T LET ME DOWN
(Apple 2490) May 1969

THE BALLAD OF JOHN AND YOKO/OLD BROWN SHOE
(Apple 2531) June 1969

SOMETHING/COME TOGETHER
(Apple 2654) October 1969

LET IT BE/YOU KNOW MY NAME (LOOK UP THE NUMBER)
(Apple 2764) March 1970

THE LONG AND WINDING ROAD/FOR YOU BLUE
(Apple 2832) May 1970

THE BEATLES AMERICAN ALBUMS

INTRODUCING THE BEATLES

I Saw Her Standing There/Misery/Anna/Chains/Boys/Love Me Do
P.S. I Love You/Baby It's You/Do You Want To Know A Secret
A Taste Of Honey/There's A Place/Twist And Shout
(Vee Jay VJLP 1062) July 1963

MEET THE BEATLES

I Want To Hold Your Hand/I Saw Her Standing There/This Boy
It Won't Be Long/All I've Got To Do/All My Loving/Don't Bother
Me/Little Child/Till There Was You/Hold Me Tight
I Wanna Be Your Man/Not A Second Time
(Capitol T 2047, mono; ST 2047, stereo) January 1964

INTRODUCING THE BEATLES

Reissue of earlier album of same title, with Ask Me Why and
Please Please Me replacing Love Me Do and P.S. I Love You
(Vee Jay VJLP 1062) January 1964

THE BEATLES WITH TONY SHERIDAN & THEIR GUESTS

My Bonnie/Cry For A Shadow/The Saints/Why
(plus eight tracks not by The Beatles)
(MGM SE 4215) February 1964

JOLLY WHAT! THE BEATLES & FRANK IFIELD ON STAGE

Please Please Me/From Me To You/Ask Me Why/Thank You Girl
(plus eight tracks by Frank Ifield)
(Vee Jay VJLP 1085) February 1964

THE BEATLES' SECOND ALBUM

Roll Over Beethoven/Thank You Girl/You Really Got A Hold On
Me/Devil In Her Heart/Money/You Can't Do That/Long Tall Sally
I Call Your Name/Please Mr Postman/I'll Get You/She Loves You
(Capitol T 2080, mono; ST 2080, stereo) April 1964

A HARD DAY'S NIGHT

A Hard Day's Night/Tell Me Why/I'll Cry Instead
I'm Happy Just To Dance With You/I Should Have Known Better
If I Fell/And I Love Her/Can't Buy Me Love
(plus four tracks by George Martin and his Orchestra)
(United Artists UAS 6366) June 1964

SOMETHING NEW

I'll Cry Instead/Things We Said Today/Anytime At All/When I Get
Home/Slow Down/Matchbox/Tell Me Why/And I Love Her/I'm Happy
Just To Dance With You/If I Fell/Komm Gib Mir Deine Hand
(Capitol T 2108. mono; ST 2108, stereo) July 1964

THE BEATLES VS. THE FOUR SEASONS

(double album)
Contains one album with the same tracks as the second issue of
'Introducing The Beatles', plus one album by The Four Seasons
(Vee Jay VJDX 30) October 1964

AIN'T SHE SWEET

Ain't She Sweet/Sweet Georgia Brown/Take Out Some Insurance On Me
Baby/Nobody's Child (plus eight tracks by The Swallows)
(Atco SD 33-169) October 1964

SONGS, PICTURES AND STORIES OF THE FABULOUS BEATLES

Same tracks as second issue of 'Introducing The Beatles'
(Vee Jay VJLP 1092) October 1964

THE BEATLES' STORY

(double album documentary)
On Stage With The Beatles/How Beatlemania Began/Beatlemania In
Action/Man Behind The Beatles; Brian Epstein/John Lennon/Who's A
Millionaire?/Beatles Will Be Beatles/Man Behind The Music: George
Martin/George Harrison/A Hard Day's Night – Their First Movie
Paul McCartney/Sneaky Haircuts And More About Paul/Twist And Shout
(live)/The Beatles Look At Life/Victims Of Beatlemania
Beatle Medley/Ringo Starr/Liverpool And All Over The World!
(Capitol STBO 2222) November 1964

BEATLES '65

No Reply/I'm A Loser/Baby's In Black/Rock And Roll Music
I'll Follow The Sun/Mr Moonlight/Honey Don't/I'll Be Back
She's A Woman/I Feel Fine/Everybody's Trying To Be My Baby
(Capitol T 2228, mono; ST 2228, stereo) December 1964

THE EARLY BEATLES

Love Me Do/Twist And Shout/Anna/Chains/Boys/Ask Me Why
Please Please Me/P.S. I Love You/Baby It's You/A Taste Of Honey
Do You Want To Know A Secret
(Capitol T 2309, mono; ST 2358, stereo) March 1965

BEATLES VI

Kansas City; Hey Hey Hey Hey/Eight Days A Week/You Like Me Too
Much/Bad Boy/I Don't Want To Spoil The Party/Words Of Love
What You're Doing/Yes It Is/Dizzy Miss Lizzy
Tell Me What You See/Every Little Thing
(Capitol T 2358, mono; ST 2358, stereo) June 1965

HELP!

Help!/The Night Before/You've Got To Hide Your Love Away
I Need You/Another Girl/Ticket To Ride/Your Going To Lose That Girl
(plus six tracks of incidental music)
(Capitol MAS 2386, mono; SMAS 2386, stereo) August 1965

RUBBER SOUL

I've Just Seen A Face/Norwegian Wood/You Won't See Me
Think For Yourself/The Word/Michelle/It's Only Love/Girl
I'm Looking Through You/In My Life/Wait/Run For Your Life
(Capitol T 2442, mono; ST 2442, stereo) December 1965

YESTERDAY & TODAY
Drive My Car/I'm Only Sleeping/Nowhere Man/Dr Robert/Yesterday/Act Naturally/And Your Bird Can Sing
If I Needed Someone/We Can Work It Out/What Goes On/Day Tripper
(Capitol T 2553, mono; ST 2553, stereo) June 1966

REVOLVER
Taxman/Eleanor Rigby/Love You To/Here, There And Everywhere/Yellow Submarine/She Said She Said/Good Day Sunshine
For No One/Dr Robert/I Want To Tell You
Got To Get You Into My Life/Tomorrow Never Knows
(Capitol T 2576, mono; ST 2576, stereo) August 1966

THIS IS WHERE IT STARTED
My Bonnie/Cry For A Shadow/The Saints/Why
(plus six tracks not by The Beatles)
(Metro MS 563) August 1966

THE AMAZING BEATLES & OTHER GREAT ENGLISH GROUP SOUNDS
Ain't She Sweet/Take Out Some Insurance On Me Baby
Nobody's Child/Sweet Georgia Brown (plus six tracks not by The Beatles)
(Clarion 601) October 1966

SGT. PEPPER'S LONELY HEARTS CLUB BAND
Same tracks as British album
(Capitol MAS 2653, mono; SMAS 2653, stereo) June 1967

MAGICAL MYSTERY TOUR
Magical Mystery Tour/The Fool On The Hill/Flying/Blue Jay Way
Your Mother Should Know/I Am The Walrus/Hello Goodbye/Strawberry Fields Forever/Penny Lane/Baby You're A Rich Man/All You Need Is Love
(Capitol MAL 2835, mono; SMAL 2835, stereo) November 1967

THE BEATLES
(double album)
Same tracks as British album
(Apple SWBO 101) November 1968

YELLOW SUBMARINE
Same tracks as British album
(Apple SW 153) January 1969

ABBEY ROAD
Same tracks as British album
(Apple SO 383) October 1969

HEY JUDE
(also released as 'The Beatles Again')
Can't Buy Me Love/I Should Have Known Better
Paperback Writer/Rain/Lady Madonna/Revolution/Hey Jude
Old Brown Shoe/Don't Let Me Down/The Ballad Of John And Yoko
(Apple SW 385) February 1970

IN THE BEGINNING-' CIRCA 1960
Same tracks as 'The Beatles First' album
(Polydor 24-4504) May 1970

LET IT BE
Same tracks as British album
(Apple AR 34001) May 1970

THE BEATLES AT THE HOLLYWOOD BOWL
Same tracks as British album
(Capitol SMAS 11638) May 1977

THE BEATLES LIVE AT THE STAR CLUB HAMBURG, GERMANY, 1962
(double album)
I'm Gonna Sit Right Down And Cry/Roll Over Beethoven/Hippy Hippy Shake/Sweet Little Sixteen/Lend Me Your Comb/Your Feet's Too Big/Where Have You Been All My Life/Mr Moonlight/A Taste Of Honey/Besame Mucho/Till There Was You/Kansas City; Hey Hey Hey Hey/Nothin' Shakin'/To Know Her Is To Love Her/Little Queenie/Falling In Love Again/Sheila/Be-Bop-A-Lula/Hallelujah I Love Her So/Red Sails In The Sunset/Everybody's Trying To Be My Baby/Matchbox/I'm Talking About You/Shimmy Shake/Long Tall Sally/I Remember You
(Lingasong LS2 7001) June 1977

THE COMPLETE SILVER BEATLES
Same tracks as British album
(Audio Rarities AR 2452) September 1982

THE SILVER BEATLES VOLUME 1
Three Cool Cats (extended)/Memphis Tennessee (extended)/Besame Mucho/The Sheik Of Araby/Till There Was You/Searching (extended)
Sure To Fall (extended) (extended tracks were edited versions of originals)
(Phoenix-10 PHX 352) September 1982

THE SILVER BEATLES VOLUME 2
Searching (extended)/Take Good Care Of My Baby (extended)
Money (extended)/To Know Her Is To love Her
Three Cool Cats (extended)/September In The Rain (extended)
Crying, Waiting, Hoping (extended tracks were edited versions of originals)
(Phoenix-10 PHX 353) September 1982